Overcoming

Overcoming addictions

How to break the habits that could be damaging your health

by
Janet Pleshette

Thorsons Publishing Group

First published 1989

© Janet Pleshette 1989

British Library Cataloguing in Publication Data

Pleshette, Janet
Overcoming addictions
1. Addiction.   Therapy
1. Title
616.86′06

ISBN 0-7225-1591-X

Published by Thorsons Publishers Limited,
Wellingborough, Northamptonshire, NN8 2RQ, England

Printed in Great Britain by Billing & Sons Limited, Worcester

1 3 5 7 9 10 8 6 4 2

Contents

To Pon, Kin, the kids, and John.

'Addiction is now recognized officially as one of the world's greatest social problems – possibly affecting as many people as the common cold. Although we never mind admitting to having a cold, very few of us are prepared to admit being an addict.'

Hooked? Meg Patterson, MBE, MBchB, FRCSE
(Faber and Faber, 1986).

Author's note

Here is a range of alternative, or complementary, approaches to giving up several addictive substances. These methods can make withdrawing easier and sometimes quicker and they will improve your health at the same time. But they are only part of your recovery. The longest and most complex task is staying off, and the most important step is the first one, which no therapy (and no other person) can do for you. That step is deciding to stop.

Foreword

It is all very well to counsel people who are in need of help to take responsibility for their own lives and improve their health, but the major issue is, How?

Janet Pleshette has written a super book in answer to this question for those of us who are troubled with addictions – from cigarettes and coffee, to alcohol, cocaine and tranquillizers. Janet Pleshette not only informs her readers about the nature of addictive illness, its causes and treatments, she also examines specific addictions in depth and explores natural and alternative remedies for helping them. She then goes on to list centres for alternative treatments throughout Britain and Ireland so that anyone looking for help has a pocket guide for where to find it.

Like all of Janet Pleshette's books, this one is authoritative and admirably researched. I am delighted to see it made available, for it will be a godsend to many people in desperate need of help. I hope we will see many more like it covering other health problems in the future, their possible solutions, and places where those in need can go for help.

Leslie Kenton
1988

Introduction

The word 'addiction' comes from the Latin word 'addicere', one meaning of which is 'to surrender'. We can surrender ourselves to anything, and be unable to do without it. It can be a hard drug, such as heroin, or an accepted everyday drug, such as the caffeine in coffee, or it can be an activity: gambling, watching television, even falling in love. The problem is not the heroin, or the innocuous cup of coffee, or being enamoured of someone. The problem is our overriding, obsessive need to repeat the experience, even when to do so damages us.

For, to begin with, it is the *experience* which gets us hooked. Heroin gives euphoria and freedom from anxiety; coffee gives a boost of energy; and falling in love a marvellous high. When we feel we must repeat the experience to the exclusion of all else, we are addicted.

This book is about substance addiction – substances which influence the mood, either stimulating or sedating us. Addiction can be both psychological and physical. If we think we can't be happy or function well without our substance, this is psychological dependency; different from, but usually accompanying, physical dependency. When every cell in the body craves the drug, this is physical dependency.

If the drug is withdrawn, mind and body usually react. The person feels unbalanced – or suffers far more severely – as he or she faces each moment without the beloved substance which has helped, and damaged, him so much. The addict's knowledge that he has been harming himself is swamped by his longing for another fix. Over time, the addiction has him at its mercy. With control over his life slipping away, he loses confidence and self-respect.

Tranquillizers and heroin can take away a person's individuality and turn him into a zombie. Addiction can damage his physical health, too, to an appalling extent; a body cannot be healthy if it is dependent upon a drug. Most drugs weaken the immune system, which fights infection, and, of course, even a single heroin injection with an infected needle can transmit AIDS.

When the drug wears off, the addict is faced once more with the grey realities of life, the conflicts and the long stretches of anxiety or fatigue that were there before. He has not progressed towards solving any problems. He has simply slipped a little further away from grappling with them.

The addiction boom

Addiction is not new. The priests of ancient civilizations used herbs to influence mood and induce mystic states. From primitive people vacantly chewing betel nut to the Victorians with their taste for laudanum, we have always had addictions. It is the *scale* of the current problem which is frightening.

Western society has a drugs epidemic on its hands. At least five per cent of the UK workforce drinks too much. (Doctors lead the country in alcoholism; one estimate puts the number with drink problems at between 2,000 and 4,000.) About half a million people in the UK are addicted to tranquillizers. Since 1971 the numbers of hard-drug addicts known to the Home Office have increased by two-and-a-half times (14,768 in 1986) and these figures are only part of the real total. Marks and Spencer are among the firms which run addiction units for their employees, and cocaine use is common now in the City of London.

Drugs are easy to get. Alcohol and tobacco are on sale in supermarkets, and heroin and cocaine are almost as easy to buy. London is still the major UK drug centre, but street use is spreading in other cities, particularly where there is high unemployment. Illegal drugs are transported round the world, making fortunes for their dealers.

The addicts

The substances people generally get addicted to are those which are closest to hand. The bored housewife in her automated kitchen or the show-business executive may both depend on alcohol. The single parent in a tower block may get the shakes without Valium. The office worker who drinks 12 cups of coffee a day and the rock star polishing his image with cocaine are both addicts.

Even an unborn baby can be addicted if his mother uses drugs, many of which can cross the placental barrier. Teenagers are open to social pressure from friends to experiment with drugs; they may see this as living with style, risk and glamour. They're certainly right about the risk. Or they may simply be following their parents' example; a chain-smoking father who fights with his son because he is taking heroin while upstairs mother is full of sleeping pills, is on a sticky wicket.

Why do we get addicted?

We are all potential addicts. Some of us have addictions which are socially acceptable, such as television, coffee, or even aerobics and jogging, which are more positive. So we don't need to feel ashamed of them. There is no sharp dividing line between the telly addict and the heroin addict; it's just a question of degree. Although most of us are addicts, however mildly, at some point in our lives, we usually manage to avoid that crippling dependency which destroys health and distorts life.

I talked to several practitioners with experience in treating addiction, and everything that they said pointed to one thing – that addiction arises from need; that it serves a purpose. The imperative that turns a relatively harmless substance – say, alcohol, or sugar – into an addictant, that gives us more than a passing acquaintance with heroin or cocaine, is inside ourselves.

Addiction fills a gap of one kind or another. One gap is fatigue. Low vitality, or health which is slightly under par, make us reach for that cup of strong tea or coffee which will lift us, give us a boost for an hour or so. This is also true of sugar.

Another gap is created through loneliness, grief or worry; we long to be relieved of the burden. Others constantly have to battle with chronic tension and a fear of life. So we reach for the bottle of tranquillizers. Alcohol makes us feel, perhaps only for the moment, witty and relaxed. Tobacco and heroin iron out anxiety, and cocaine brings feelings of confidence and energy.

It is indeniably pleasant to be able to manipulate ourselves with drugs sometimes, in a harmless way. Wine is a delightful companion at a dinner party and coffee at the end of a busy morning's shopping is a good reviver. Tranquillizers can lend a helping hand sometimes during a time of shock and crisis. The problem arises when we cannot do without them.

Many reasons are offered for the additional need that pushes someone over into addiction. One is a feeling of inner emptiness, a sense of being generally useless and of not counting for much – of being a failure. As one young woman who was addicted to heroin said, with heart-breaking candour, 'I am a great disappointment to myself.'

For some addicts, particularly heroin addicts, life was pretty dull in the first place. One user, asked why he started, replied, 'There just wasn't anything else to do.' An addict's first experience of illegal drug-taking may happen because everyone else was trying it and he or she didn't want to be left out. Or, among the very rich, drugs may give the kicks they cannot get in any other way.

Addicts can have difficult family backgrounds. Healer Ian G (Directory: Halsey Street, London SW3) says, 'A common thread I find running through most addictions is a very difficult relationship with parents. I think in many cases there has been pressure on a child to do something he's just not capable of, or it's not the right path for him to follow, so he feels a failure. A feeling of failure is the most common thing amongst addicts.'

Scottish surgeon Meg Patterson, who has had years of experience in treating heroin addicts, finds that most have had a weak or absent father, unsettled homes full of anxiety, and often parents who either smoked or drank a lot. Some had a history of taking prescribed drugs before they began taking illegal ones. She feels that these intense stresses force people into searching for some relief.

However, blaming the addict's family is pretty pointless, and may not be justified in every case. In *The Times*, 15 July 1986, Griffith Edwards, Professor of Addiction Behaviour at the University of London's Institute of Psychiatry, wrote: 'The idea that every addict is by definition a person of flawed character is not only mistaken but also a potential hindrance to recovery and an added burden.'

Some people just have impossible lives. Carol W (Directory: Lisson Grove, London NW1), who has set up a treatment service for addicts, has had a lot of experience with people addicted to tranquillizers.

Mostly the women who come to us are in their thirties and have had years and years of being totally messed up. They're often very poor, in hopeless situations with young children, sometimes living on the nineteenth floor of a tower block with a husband who drinks and beats them up. Valium is a big problem, but Ativan is the worst tranquillizer drug.

People at the bottom of our society, perhaps unemployed, still have access to television. They are still bombarded with advertisements telling them that happiness means using the right soap powder, or deodorant, or driving the latest car. They are presented with seductive images of beautiful, adventurous, sexy people, for whom everything always comes out right in the end. They are puzzled and made angry by the chasm between their own struggles and all this glitter, and they may seek a way out in drugs.

Some of us first encounter addictive tranquillizers after a profound and agonizing shock: bereavement, divorce, or the break-up of our lives in some other way – almost unbearable stresses that can be alleviated by a timely prescription. A woman's child died, and she became addicted to Valium. Years later, when she finally came off the drug, the grief that had been repressed by it finally came to the surface and had to be lived through.

Addiction is also thought to be an attempt to escape from 'modern stress'. But what about medieval stress, when there was no unemployment benefit, and you could lose a hand for stealing a loaf of bread? Perhaps what we have nowadays is not more stress, just more chemical ways of escaping from it.

It is also true that, for many of us now, God has receded or is dead. Instead of the framework that established religion gave us, we are on our own. Some people are filling this gap with a variety of freer, more inspirational religious pathways, but another way to fill it is with drugs. 'I believe that drug-taking is a sign of a very deep need,' Carol W told me. 'In a society whose religious thrust is completely gone, like ours, what *do* people cling to?'

Conventional treatments

There is a nationwide network of agencies and treatment centres to combat addiction; please see the first section of the Directory.

Treatments fall into three broad categories:

- Hospital in-patient detoxification
- Drug dependency units which treat out-patient groups and where counselling and advice are also available
- Maintenance doses of the addictant drug, or a replacement drug, prescribed by a doctor to his patient who is living and working in the community.

Drugs used as substitutes are said to help 'detoxify' the addict of his original substance. Unfortunately, however, 'detoxify' is the last thing they do. I have dealt with the side-effects and addictive nature of methadone, antabuse and several other drug 'cures' in the sections dealing with the drug whose use they replace or discourage. Dr Patterson sounds a warning 'against the present use of addictive drugs by doctors in drug and alcohol treatment centres – which make as many addicts as they cure.'[1]

Many authorities are not happy about maintenance prescribing; the *Evening Standard* newspaper recently (4 August 1987) criticized a Harley Street doctor who simply signs prescriptions for continuous long-use of the addictant, thus making life much easier for the addict (providing he is happy to go on being an addict).

Counselling is widely available in the drug treatment centres, and all the practitioners I spoke to emphasized the urgent need for, and the value of, this kind of help, especially when someone is coming off one of the dangerously addictive drugs.

The problem with the present overall policy is that, in spite of the efforts and money being poured into it, it often does not work, and the addict goes back to his addiction. In her book *Hooked?*[1] Dr Patterson writes: 'The official reluctance to underwrite any realistic efforts to tackle the scale of the drug explosion is exacerbated by the tragic waste of resources which are channelled towards ineffective "cures".'

Drugless ways of treating addiction

In the following pages I describe the main treatments in this field. The practitioners I spoke to repeatedly said that they try to treat the whole person – body, mind and spirit – and reach the underlying cause of his or her addiction. Getting the patient drug-free must also include alleviating his withdrawal symptoms and enhancing his general health as well so that he will eventually be able to face life without the drug.

One of the first practitioners I interviewed was an acupuncturist. 'We do not attempt to suppress desires by the use of acupuncture', he told me, 'but rather to balance a person's meridians at the three levels of body, mind and spirit so that he is less likely to need props to help him cope with life.' (To consult this practitioner, please see Directory: Whitehall Road, Norwich, Norfolk.)

Addiction is believed to develop more easily in a malnourished body; junk food can unbalance a person's metabolism so that he feels he must stimulate his flagging energies or sedate his starving nervous system with drugs. Most practitioners use nutrition as part of their treatment:

I always carry out a nutritional assessment first, said Dr S (Directory: 138 Harley Street, London W1), together with hair analysis, and I prepare special vitamin and mineral supplements for each individual patient.

I don't tackle addiction head-on; I tackle it from the point of view of how the person got addicted in the first place. Why? Why does he need this harmful thing?

The person has to be completely transformed – from ill-health, addiction, to well-being and lack of addiction. This transformation needs a lot of energy, and it is here that the energy-based therapies – acupuncture in its various forms, homoeopathy, ultra-sound – are the most helpful. The person doesn't have this energy to start with. He knows the substance is bad for him but he says, 'I can't stop.' Coming off is uphill and a car cannot go uphill unless you change gear. What is required, therefore, is more energy.

I am changing the reaction to the substance, instead of simply making the patient avoid it. When I change this reaction, the problem of addiction isn't there any more; there is a gradual lessening of the urge. The patient will say, for example, 'Yes, I still like sweets. But the need for sweets has gone; and this goes for the dangerous drugs, too.

He understands that the addict often doesn't want to come out from under his addiction. 'They are afraid to change; they hang on to their addiction. It's an anchor. The change is fearful.' He believes that our modern wave of drug addiction is part of contemporary unease. 'I think that we are looking for our own identity and that this search is deeply disturbing and is too much for some people.'

Sylvia B, healer (Directory: 15 Ann Lane, London SW10), agrees that addiction is an attempt to deal with some form of unhappiness.

Personal, business problems, being generally out of harmony with yourself; I call this dis-easement. I think that people get addicted to drink or drugs and a way of living that isn't good for them, partly as a cry for help, but mostly as a way out. They don't know any other way. There has to be a lot of counselling and encouraging someone to talk about what's really happening deep down inside them; that's the beginning of healing. The answer to any stress, depression, hurt, is to find the peace within you and live in harmony. It isn't easy, even when you've found it.

I know there's a power that we call God; it doesn't matter what it's called. It's the universal creative force, universal love. After all, you can't see love, you can't chart it. You only know that you can cope with anything if you feel that you are loved.

Research into Transcendental Meditation (TM) shows that this is an effective way of getting off drugs; confrontations with the fact of addiction are not part of this approach either. Mr W, an accountant and latterly a teacher of TM, wrote to me: 'I was . . . addicted to Valium in 1973 when I learned TM. Three months later I stopped using tranquillizers and I have never resumed. I also stopped using tobacco, alcohol and coffee. It was all very easy and natural . . . The resolution of addictions is just one of the many "by-products" of this excellent technique.'

Getting off and staying off

Some people manage to come off drugs quite easily; we don't all suffer agonizing withdrawal symptoms. A few addictive substances – caffeine and sugar, for example – are less harmful anyway and much easier to give up.

However, for those having problems, those for whom this book is written, there are three stages to go through:

● Having faced the fact that you have an addiction, or at least a dependency, making the decision to overcome it

- Alone, or with the help of a practitioner, withdrawing from the addictant
- Making any life changes necessary for you to remain substance-free. Your body can take up to two years to purge itself of every sign of some drugs; this applies to heroin, tranquillizers, alcohol and nicotine.

Making the decision

You must *want* to give it up.

This may seem a pretty obvious point to make, but the resolution may not be there. People least likely to have made it are those persuaded to seek help by family and friends, but who are not really convinced themselves that the time is ripe. 'You have to find out if people are ready,' said acupuncturist Caroline K (Directory: Barbican, London EC2), 'Very often, they are not. They will come to me saying that they want to stop, but that's not what they mean at all; they are only trying to find a way of controlling it, maintaining it, giving themselves a bit of space.'

Some people will seek treatment without intending to make any effort themselves. Acupuncturist and homoeopath Evonne F (Directory: Victoria Road, London NW6) has tried to help people like this.

That sort of person will come to you, saying 'This is my ailment – let me know when you've treated it. In the meantime, I will drink any amount of booze instead of the drug, I'll go to bed at 3 a.m., I'll abuse myself in various other ways but I still want you to get me well.' There are a lot of people like that – openly or unconsciously with that attitude.

If you decide to try one of the alternative, or complementary, therapies described in this book, please bear the following points in mind:

- Choose a therapy you feel will be right for you. Be prepared to ask questions, both about the treatment and the practitioner's qualifications and experience (see first section of the directory for information)
- Find a therapist who is reasonably accessible for you
- Do not be afraid to combine certain approaches – for instance, most hard drug addicts find coming off easier if they seek some kind of counselling, or the friendly support of others going through the same process

- Your doctor might find it interesting to know about your treatment (in any case, many of those listed in the Directory are doctors). Many GPs now are very interested in, and open-minded about, the alternative field
- Most alternative medicine has to be paid for. If you are in financial difficulties, please see the Concessions Register in the first section of the Directory – but bear in mind that the fees quoted are only estimates; many practitioners asked me to say that they will reduce fees in some circumstances
- Remember that your recovery depends largely on your co-operation; if your practitioner gives you nutritional advice, for example, then you must stick to it. And, of course, the path out of addiction, however much help you get, ultimately depends on you.

Withdrawing

We are afraid of giving up the beloved substance, of going through the pain of withdrawing. Naturopath and osteopath Susan T (Directory: Meopham, Kent) believes that she only sees those who are committed to coming off, but even so, 'When a person is withdrawing, in the initial stages they might say, "Oh, why am I bothering with all this? I'll go back on it! I can't be bothered to keep off!"' She sees her part during this stage as 'galvanizing the will so that they can stick to the treatment and the routine. My job is to get them to the point where they don't need me any more.' She has found that a person who is addicted is particularly sensitive; his mind and body are in a state of irritability. 'That's why it's so difficult to kick addiction.'

We also fear the emptiness afterwards, and the changes we may have to make to our lives in order to stay off. Medical herbalist Julian B (Directory: Wilbury Road, Hove, Sussex) agrees. 'If you give up a drug, you then have to learn to do without it. What are you going to do? It's the required dragon. It's actually guarding the gate you don't want to go through.'

Some heavy drug users may be severely damaged, so that giving up the drug is made even more difficult. Carol W found that some tranquilliser addicts suffer from short-term memory loss, so that even turning up for treatment is an ordeal.

One problem with tranquillizer addicts is that they are not here. One woman who comes in to see me has to write the address down on a bit of paper and hold it in her hand because 20 or 30 times on the way here she forgets what she is doing and has to look at it.

Alternative therapies – acupuncture, herbal medicine, homoeopathy and others – can minimize the discomfort experienced during withdrawal and enhance the patient's vitality so that he is in a better shape to stay off. And, of course, they don't replace one drug with another.

Please see the Directory for a nationwide list of alternative practitioners and clinics able to treat addiction.

Making changes

The changes you will have to make in your life depend on the drug you have been using and the way you live now.

For example, addicts of heroin and cocaine are usually part of a network of users and they will find it necessary to make other contacts to replace those they have had to give up.

People with a drinking problem will either have to avoid wine bars and pubs, or choose alcohol-free or alcohol-reduced drinks.

Someone on tranquillizers is in a different situation again. He or she was probably not part of a group of users, and the change needed may not be to give up old friends, but to make entirely new ones.

I have described the help available to each drug user in the section devoted to that particular drug, and also in the directory.

Any re-structuring of your life is going to take determination and self-discipline. However, life changes always work better when you don't worry about gritting your teeth and forcing yourself, but simply organize your life in a different way, creating the self-management which will make it possible for you to develop a better way of living. You might, for instance, join a support group or deliberately practise a relaxation technique.

A necessity for you now is increased self-esteem. As you cut down or give up, reward yourself. One practitioner told me that she always asks the patients who are coming off tranquillizers to spend a little time each day indulging themselves. So, whatever you enjoy, try to fit it into your life; this is the time for new interests and plenty of healthy hedonism. Don't knock yourself. Appreciate your accomplishments – in particular the terrific achievement of coming off drugs. If you relapse occasionally, forgive yourself. We all backslide, all the time.

Healer Ian G has a high opinion of ex-addicts.

> *I do believe that you can pass through the tunnel of addiction. Some people describe it as spiritual bankruptcy and, when they work it all out, this bankruptcy can develop into a tremendous spiritual power and strength. Therefore I think that among addicts there is a great potential for good. They can be wonderful people, if they work it all through.*

You must always remember that there is no addiction that has not been beaten, somewhere, by someone who was just as full of doubts and fears as you are.

Reference

1 *Hooked? NET: The new approach to drug cure*, by Meg Patterson (Faber and Faber, 1986).

Part One
Substances

Alcohol

Alcoholic drinks have been with us since our primitive beginnings. Wine is taken for granted throughout the world and paintings show the god Bacchus, garlanded with flowers and tipsy, but unharmed. A daily glass of wine is associated with a decreased risk of heart disease and St Paul tells us 'Take a little wine for thy stomach's sake.'

But, in excess, alcohol is a toxic and addictive drug. According to ACCEPT, the drink-abuse charity, alcoholism is 'our third major health hazard after heart disease and cancer. Continued alcohol misuse may lead to social, legal, domestic, job and financial problems. It may also cut lifespan by 10 to 15 years and lead to overdosing, suicide, accidents and deaths from drunken driving.'[1]

We drink partly because we like what it does to us. Drinking can be part of a celebration – a wedding or a party – and it makes us feel friendly, cheerful and uninhibited. On these occasions, a drink is clearly a pleasant social habit. In a crisis, it appears to steady our nerves by damping down anxiety or shock. The alcoholic drinks, however, because he or she can't stop.

A bottle of wine used to be a luxury. Now, more and more people are taking wine with their meals as a matter of course. Liberalization of the drinking laws, both now and in the 1960s, has made the liquor business boom. The biggest growth in the market has been among women; they meet in pubs and wine bars and pick a bottle off the supermarket shelves with the shopping. Television emphasizes snobbery and style to sell wine and a macho, aggressive image for beer and lager, and the Campaign for Real Ale is encouraging more middle-class people to drink beer. Drinkers are getting younger, too. A recent government survey found that 52 per cent of boys and 37 per cent of girls aged 15 were drinking regularly.

Figures on alcoholism are part of these rising trends. ACCEPT estimates that about 750,000 people in the UK are seriously dependent on alcohol and another 650,000 have a drinking problem. In its recent report, *A Great and Growing Evil*,[2] the Royal College of Physicians states that there are now about 40,000 alcohol-related deaths every year.

Alcohol and health

Most of us who enjoy the occasional drink will not get addicted. But anyone who drinks so much that it interferes with health, relationships and work has a drinking problem, which may develop into alcoholism.

According to the Health Education Council publication *That's the Limit* any man who drinks more than eight units of alcohol a day (see chart) is drinking too much and may damage his health. A woman who is drinking more than three units a day may be in danger of damaging her health.

A hangover gives us well-known symptoms: headache, fatigue, dizziness, nausea, vomiting and thirst. But we can recover. Long-term heavy drinking, however, does not simply make the person feel terrible for a few hours. It damages all the tissues and systems in the body.

The liver is the principal victim. It is the liver which metabolizes alcohol and tries to use it as a food and turn it into energy. But if someone drinks too much the liver eventually gets swamped and cannot cope. First, it builds tolerance to the alcohol, producing more enzymes to handle it, but most drinkers develop a fatty, enlarged liver and, as liver damage progresses, its capacity is impaired and less alcohol is needed to get drunk. Liver damage from alcohol can lead to a fatty liver or to cirrhosis, alcoholic hepatitis and liver failure with jaundice. Alcoholics also have a higher incidence of liver cancer. Cirrhosis – the dead liver cells, massive scarring and fibrous tissue which develops in 10 to 30 per cent of heavy drinkers – deforms the liver and can eventually be fatal.

The brain is also vulnerable to alcohol abuse, which destroys brain cells. Research at a Veterans' Administration Hospital in the US found that the brains of alcoholics were ageing faster, and seemed, effectively, to be ten years older than

Alcohol content of various beverages

Beverage	grams of alcohol	units of alcohol
Beers and lagers		
ordinary strength beer or	8 g/½ pint	1
lager	12 g/can	1.5
(3% alcohol)	16 g/pint	2
export beer	16 g/can	2
(4% alcohol)	20 g/pint	2.5
strong beer or lager	16 g/½ pint	2
(5.5% alcohol)	24 g/can	3
	32 g/pint	4
extra strength beer or lager	20 g/½ pint	2.5
(7% alcohol)	32 g/can	4
	40 g/pint	5
Ciders		
average cider	12 g/½ pint	1.5
(4% alcohol)	24 g/pint	3
strong cider	16 g/½ pint	2
(6% alcohol)	32 g/pint	4
	64 g/quart bottle	8
Spirits		
whisky 70 proof	8 g/single measure	
(32% alcohol)	in England and Wales	1
or		
brandy 70 proof	12 g/single measure	
(32% alcohol)	in Scotland and N. Ireland	1.5
or		
whisky 70 proof	240g/bottle	30
(32% alcohol)		
or		
vodka 70 proof	240g/bottle	30
(32% alcohol)		
or		
gin 70 proof	240g/bottle	30
(32% alcohol)		
Table wines		
(8-10% alcohol)	8 g/standard glass	1
	56 g/bottle	7
	100 g/litre bottle	12.5
Fortified wine		
sherry		
port	8 g/standard measure	1
Vermouth	120 g/bottle	15
(13-16% alcohol)		
Liqueurs		
(15-30% alcohol)	8 g/small measure	1
	100-240g/bottle	12.5-30

Taken from *A Great and Growing Evil: The medical consequences of alcohol abuse* (Tavistock Publications, 1987).

Chart reproduced by kind permission of Tavistock Publications Ltd.

the brains of non-alcoholics of the same age.[3] Brain deterioration causes bad judgement, memory lapses and inability to concentrate, as well as depression, anxiety and nervousness. Prolonged alcoholism can lead to other serious brain disorders, and result in violent behaviour, dementia, epilepsy and hallucinations. More crimes and accidents take place under the influence of alcohol, and suicides are between 20 and 60 times more common.[2]

The heavy drinker often suffers from malnutrition, both because he prefers alcohol to food, and because damage to the digestive tract interferes with nutrient absorption. Alcoholic gastritis can cause anorexia, nausea, vomiting and diarrhoea, with damage to the oesophagus (food pipe), and can produce stomach ulcers. Gums can become swollen and bleed, and often saliva thickens. Alcohol is a major cause of inflammation of the pancreas, found in at least 40 per cent of alcoholic patients;[4] this can cause a severe drop in blood sugar and eventual diabetes.

The progressive malnutrition associated with alcoholism affects the whole body. Alcoholics lack vitamin B_1 and can even get beri-beri, a sign of extreme B_1 deficiency. A shortage of folic acid may result in folic acid anaemia and 50 per cent of alcoholics lack B_6.[2] A lesser-known B vitamin, choline, which is made by the liver under the right conditions, works with inositol to break up liver fat, and a choline deficiency can lead to cirrhosis.[5]

Alcoholism also depletes B_2, B_3, B_6, and B_{12}, which are all needed for energy, brain function, sound nerves and good digestion. It causes deficiencies of calcium and magnesium – essential for a healthy heart and sound nerves – and zinc, without which a damaged liver cannot regenerate new cells.[6] It increases the need for vitamin C, the anti-stress and anti-illness vitamin.

Heavy drinking lessens the effectiveness of an essential fatty acid (EFA), linoleic acid. This substance is needed both to make lecithin, which washes away excess fats, and as the first step in the manufacture of other EFAs which in their turn help energy production, immunity, good circulation and healthy skin and hair. The last step in this complex process is the manufacture of prostaglandins which are are work in almost every cell in the body.

A heavy drinker is more likely to have a damaged heart and suffer a heart attack. Drinking a lot when you are not used to it can depress the contraction and strength of the heart muscle, and binges can cause abnormal heart rhythms. Strokes are three times more common in heavy drinkers. Damage to the circulation can cause neuritis and numb or tingling fingers, and there are risks of anaemia, impaired blood clotting and haemorrhages.

Another risk, over-production of the stress hormone cortisol, can cause obesity, acne, increased facial hair and high blood pressure; a Lancet study[7] found that 45 per cent of patients drinking more than two-and-a-half units a day had hypertension, which rose with the amount of alcohol taken. Too much alcohol can also impair kidney function, cause kidney infections and increase the risk of bronchitis, emphysema and lung cancer, probably due to the fact that most heavy drinkers also smoke a lot.[8] It can affect the thyroid gland too, causing over-activity, with weight loss, palpitations, tremors and sweating.[2]

Older people are often less able to drink without getting drunk; the amount of water in their bodies, which dilutes the alcohol, decreases with age.

Men and women

Men usually drink to be more sociable; some women on the other hand shut themselves up at home and drink because they are depressed.

The male hormone, testosterone, is eliminated more quickly in heavy drinkers and less is produced. The male heavy drinker can therefore suffer loss of libido and potency, with diminished or absent sperm formation and shrinking of the testes and penis; he may even eventually become feminized. Recent research found that even modest amounts of alcohol – in most cases four to six units a day – can affect male reproductive function. Of the 67 men tested, 26 had sperm impairment thought to be related to alcohol. In about half these men, sperm became normal again three months after they had stopped drinking.[9]

Women have smaller livers, more body fat, which does not absorb alcohol, and less body fluid than men in which to dilute it, so they cannot drink as much.

In women alcoholics the female sex hormone, oestradiol, is reduced. The ovaries, breasts and external genitalia shrink and the vagina becomes dry. They can also have irregular, heavy or absent periods, and are more likely to develop breast cancer.[10]

The chromosomes holding genetic material can be altered by alcohol.

Pregnant women should not drink, especially during the first 12 weeks of pregnancy, when the heart and brain of the foetus are being formed. Women alcoholics have twice the risk of spontaneous abortion.[11] The foetus of a mother who is drinking heavily is drinking himself because alcohol passes easily through to him, but his blood levels drop more slowly than those of his mother. Alcohol is therefore very toxic to the unborn child.

The effects of Foetal Alcohol Syndrome are horrifying.[2] Babies can have stunted growth, with a smaller head and a deformed face, hands and heart. Other abnormalities include intellectual impairment and delayed development. There may be difficulty in sucking (alcohol reaches the breast milk too, although whether it is harmful or not is debatable), and focusing, and the child may develop behavioural problems, hyperactivity and a short attention span.

Alcohol and other drugs

The interactions between alcohol and other drugs are complex, little understood and can be very dangerous.

Although chronic drinkers sometimes find that a drug's effect is reduced, malnutrition and liver damage may have the opposite effect, increasing sensitivity. Occasional drinkers will probably find that alcohol mixed with other drugs is a risky experiment and that the effects of both are more potent; this is particularly true of tranquillizers.

Withdrawals

After a short binge, withdrawal symptoms last only a couple of days. The person may experience a rapid heartbeat, with tremors, sweating, a rising temperature, nausea and vomiting, and insomnia. Many people feel depressed, confused, resentful and guilty.

After long-term heavy drinking, symptoms are more severe and can last a week or longer. The alcoholic may suffer hallucinations and tremors – DTs – and a high temperature and agitation can lead to convulsions with shock which can occasionally even be fatal.

Drugs

The drugs offered by doctors to combat alcoholism are very toxic. Antabuse 200 (disulfiram, recommended by ACCEPT) is not a cure; it produces unpleasant effects when alcohol is taken as well – red eyes, flushed face, throbbing headache and fast heartbeat, dizziness, nausea, vomiting and sweating, and a fall in blood pressure. These effects are so severe that the first dose should only be given in hospital, and only small amounts of alcohol may result in heart failure, unconsciousness, convulsions, and even death.[12] This drug should be used 'with the utmost caution in patients with impaired liver or kidney function . . .',[12] which is a pity, since heavy drinkers tend to have impaired livers anyway. Side-effects from regular use, without combining it with alcohol, are indigestion, body and breath odour, drowsiness, impotence, allergic skin rashes and nerve damage. It is clear from the documented side-effects that this drug is dangerous.

The minor tranquillizers, diazepam (Valium) and lorazepam (Ativan), are often given to help a patient through his withdrawal period. For the dangers of long-term use, please see the chapter on tranquillizers.

A stronger drug used during withdrawals is Heminevrin (chlormethiazole). This is a very toxic and highly addictive drug which can cause severe depression and ACCEPT recommends that it should not normally be used for longer than a week.

Vitamins and glucose are also given to some patients.

Drugless treatments

Acupuncture

Acupuncturist Caroline K (Directory: Barbican, London EC2) praises AA and other organizations, but adds:

Not many people with an alcohol problem think of trying alternative medicine, and this is a pity. It would be very, very useful; I think they should offer acupuncture in these treatment centres, instead of giving drugs.

She realizes that people only come to her as a last resort:

By the time they come here, they have really decided that they want to give up. The situation has reached rock bottom and is so horrific that they rarely go back on this decision. So I have a patient who is very dedicated and will really stick with the treatment, especially if they are going to AA too. I really try to get them along to the meetings if they haven't started yet. They do well, provided they don't have a new crisis in the early days which just drives them straight back to drink.

Garnett S (Directory: Woodhouse Road, London N12) has also found that life crises can precipitate heavy drinking:

The drinker doesn't want reality, he is escaping, hiding, blotting his consciousness out. He has got a problem. It could be marriage, work; you've got to try and help him sort it out as well as giving acupuncture.

As well as treating the liver, he gives acupuncture, which helps the patient to regain his sense of well-being, and recommends: 'Plenty of bottled water and plenty of fresh fruit. And vitamins C and A. I give acupuncture two or three times a week to start with.'

Acupuncturist and cranial osteopath Ron K (Directory: Neal's Yard, London WC2: Shirlock Road, NW3: High Street, Edgware, Middlesex) gives his patients ear studs, and emphasizes:

It's not just a matter of treating the craving; where I put the stud in the ear depends on the weaknesses – liver, stomach, heart, sympathetic nervous system – of that individual. And I support the whole physiology, both with acupuncture and cranial osteopathy, so that the body is ticking over in a much better way.

I asked him if he treats patients who drink before arriving at his practice:

The acupuncture does work if they turn up drunk. But, obviously, the more conscious a person is, and the less toxicity he has in his body, the better.

I give a good range of vitamins and minerals. And I make them all go to AA or something like it. There's a lot of emotional and psychological work to be done, and with heavy alcohol addiction, they really need a support team.

Acupuncturist Evonne F (Directory: Victoria Avenue, London NW6) feels that all addictions start with some weakness or lack of energy:

One person will try to feel better by going for a sauna, another will go to a hot place to feel rejuvenated, and another will reach for the bottle. They are all trying to do the same thing: bring up their energy level.

Mark U (Directory: Wilbury Road, Hove, Sussex) is very aware of the close connection between addiction and allergy. 'They go hand in hand. There was one man who drank a lot of beer – an addiction – and it turned out that he was allergic to the yeast in it.' Low blood sugar, which causes fatigue, accompanies the addiction/allergy and Mark thinks that this condition is often the original reason why they start drinking.

Research reported in 1984[13] found that, out of 34 heavy drinkers, 33 were cured of their craving for alcohol by acupuncture. Research reported the following year[14] found that ear acupuncture, with small doses of anti-depressants, cut alcohol withdrawals, and that 49 per cent of the patients treated were abstinent for at least two or three months.

Cranial osteopathy

Susan T (Directory: Meopham, Kent) has helped many people who cannot stop drinking.

With cranial osteopathy you notice in a heavy drinker that the membranes of the brain are very irritated and this extends down the spinal cord. This sensitivity can, in some people, not just be due to alcohol, but to other trauma: an accident, injury at birth, an emotional shock. People who have this sensitivity are, I believe, prone to addiction. When your nervous system is irritable you crave something to make you feel better, and a cigarette, some sugar, or a drink, often seem the answer. You get an immediate short-term effect, but the long-term effect is to increase the sensitivity.

She doesn't try to get heavy drinkers to give up too soon.

You don't try to treat somebody who is still drinking; there's no point. It takes a while to quieten that sensitivity down, then you try to nourish every cell in the body and drain away toxins. I might put somebody on vitamin C, the B vitamins too, and give them evening primrose oil.

Herbal medicine

Like cranial osteopathy, herbal treatment is less well-known for addiction, but Julian B (Directory: Wilbury Road, Hove, Sussex) has treated several heavy drinkers in this way.

There is no doubt that withdrawals can be helped with herbal medicine. But it is very important that treatment comes before medication; it may not involve any medication, in fact. It may just need the pastoral part of treatment: counselling and understanding. In any case, the herbalist is trying to match the structural complexity of plants with the complexity of a person's life, and he can't do that unless he knows both well.

Homoeopathy

Homoeopath Elizabeth A (Directory: Church Street, London N16) also looks beyond the addition to the patient himself.

Rather than treating the addiction by itself we consider the whole person, taking into account his background, childhood influences and so on. We can then see a clear picture to prescribe on and to help him recover from this tendency. Homoeopathy regulates the whole person and strengthens him so that he feels stronger and better able to cope with these cravings.

Hypnotherapy

Antonia C (Directory: Rochester Square, London NW1) sees hypnotherapy as being merely a tool.

But there could be a causative factor, a reason why they become addicted in the first place. Addiction to alcohol is the most difficult one to treat; they will turn up drunk. I feel that a clinic situation is much better for them.

Nutrition

The whole subject of alcoholism and nutrition is well-documented and yet largely ignored by the medical profession.

As long ago as the 1950s, American biochemist Roger J. Williams was using nutrition to treat alcoholics. Although he understood that stress, another major factor, can literally drive you to drink (he was able to turn rats into alcoholics by jangling cowbells and flashing lights at them), he asked for nutritional guidance to be used alongside counselling. 'The psychological factors enter,' he said, 'but physiological and biochemical factors are involved too, and to be ignorant of these is to be ignorant of the disease itself.'[15]

Dr Williams used an excellent diet containing high-quality protein, dairy products, vegetables, salads and fruit, with essential fatty acids derived from oils and a wide range of supplements.

Since that time, a few other doctors and researchers – mostly American – have been studying the crucial importance that nutrition has in addictions of all kinds, including alcohol.

Biochemist Dr Leonard Mervyn states that the effects of long-term heavy drinking can be prevented by vitamins B_1, B_6, B_{12} and folic acid, as well as vitamin C. A hangover can be treated with large doses of these vitamins (10 mg of B_1 and B_6, 10 mcg of B_{12}, 200 mcg of folic acid and one to three grammes of vitamin C).[5]

Dr Abram Hoffer finds large doses of B_3 and B_6 helpful for the damage caused by alcohol, and Dr David Hawkins, again using B vitamins for alcoholism, recorded a success rate of 71 per cent.[16] High doses of niacin, or vitamin B_3, have also been proved useful.[17]

Alcohol interferes with zinc absorption and causes it to be lost from the body, but the liver needs extra zinc to detoxify itself. Zinc deficiency can lead to loss of appetite too, and this may explain why heavy drinkers have no appetite for food. In their recent book, *Nutritional Medicine*,[18] doctors Stephen Davies and Alan Stewart describe treating an alcoholic of more than 20 years with vitamins and minerals including zinc. With this treatment, his craving for alcohol disappeared.

Most people who are addicted to alcohol also suffer from low blood sugar (hypoglycaemia). Alexander Schauss, pioneer into the relationship between food and behaviour, found that 97 per cent of the alcoholics he tested had low blood sugar. By giving small, nourishing meals free from added sugars to avoid low blood sugar, Dr Russell E. Smith helped 71 per cent of his 500 patients to recover from their addiction.[16]

Perhaps the single most interesting supplement for treating the damage done by alcohol is GLA, found mostly in evening primrose oil, but also in blackcurrant seed oil and in the recently launched GLA complex.

GLA (gamma linoleic acid) is needed before the body can make key substances called prostaglandins, at least one of which is effective against alcohol-induced fatty liver. GLA cuts withdrawal symptoms and restores normal liver function.[19] Expert David Horrobin recommends four 0.5 gram capsules of evening primrose oil daily to help cut down withdrawal symptoms.[20]

The building blocks of protein, amino acids, are proving to be a new and effective treatment against many addictions. One of them, glutamine, can reduce a craving for alcohol. Cysteine can prevent alcohol-related brain and liver damage, glutathione can put right alcoholic liver, and methionine helps to detoxify the body.[21]

If you wish to try amino acid therapy, please consult a practitioner who understands it, and who can make sure that you use this new approach safely.

I hope I have shown you how valuable nutrition can be when you are trying to give up heavy drinking or recover from alcoholism. In their book, *Nutritional Medicine*,[18] doctors Stephen Davies and Alan Stewart cite one rehabilitation project where the 'sober rate' rose from 37.8 per cent to 81.3 per cent after nutritional guidance was added to the programme.

Some practitioners take a different nutritional approach. They say that, since addiction and allergy are inseparable illnesses, an alcoholic is allergic to his drinking as well as being addicted to it.

This at first seems impossible; if we are allergic to something – strawberries, or shellfish – we know it. There's no mistaking the unpleasant reactions we get. But doctors have discovered that an addict can have a hidden, or 'masked' allergy to his symptoms. Here's what happens.

When we first take an alcoholic drink, we find it unpleasant. This is the first stage in the process which can lead to a masked allergy. After this, if we keep on drinking, we get used to it. This is the stage of adaptation. During this state we feel better if we can have regular doses of the substance we both crave and are basically allergic to. We are by now addicted. The third and final stage is when the substance no longer gives us a lift, but simply makes us feel worse because we can no longer adapt to its toxic effects.

Using this approach, the allergy pioneer, Dr Richard Mackarness, treats addiction to alcohol by giving a very diluted mixture of alcohol to his patients which they can take when they need to. This mixture, acting as a 'hair of the dog', turns their craving off. Several other practitioners are using this approach; for instance, Alister B (Directory: 31, Harley Street, London W1).

We give a homoeopathic dilution in a little bottle. During the first week the person avoids the offending substance and takes a few drops whenever he feels a craving coming on. After this time, he shouldn't need it or crave it any more. If he does, he simply takes some drops. He is warned then that he must go easy on the substance – whatever it is: alcohol or tobacco. What's gone – hopefully for life – is the actual addiction.

Transcendental Meditation

TM teacher Roger L (Directory: Nationwide) warns:

Alcoholics need a lot of support; they will need to go to a group like AA as well. Alcoholism, like heroin addiction, is a lifestyle that's hard to get out of.

Even an alcoholic can meditate. It's obviously better if you meditate when you're sober, but you can meditate, say, before the first drink of the day and some time after the afternoon drinks; it smooths out the situation physiologically and psychologically so that you're much more likely to feel strong enough to come off.

When this happens, withdrawal symptoms are not so bad and it's easier to give up. The actual physical withdrawals last a short time, but it's the longer-term withdrawals, the psychological changes, which are difficult. That's where meditation really comes into its own.

Research published in the *American Journal of Psychiatry* found that, out of 126 people practising TM, 40 per cent stopped drinking after six months and 60 per cent after two to three years.[22] Other studies confirm that alcohol abuse usually stops after about two years' practice of TM.

A case history: Sally

'My father was an alcoholic and my mother popped a lot of pills, so we were an addicted family.

'Alcoholism is known as the disease of denial. I was denying myself, my very existence, from a very early age. I was very withdrawn and silent and couldn't tell anyone what I wanted or needed. I needed a lot of affection as a kid and I never got it. The only way I could get attention was by being ill, so I spent a lot of time being ill; and also talking to people who weren't there, not in the physical sense at any rate. I'm a natural psychic. That was quite horrific for me. When you try to explain to people, they don't want to know.

'Alcohol was in the house all the time; it was used very much as a medicine as well. I was probably being given drink from the age of about eight or nine. I actually started drinking myself when I was at school, at about 13 or 14. I didn't actually like booze, but I thought, "This is the way to be an adult, this is the way to be normal, like other people."

'I went straight into the BBC from school. I knew exactly what I was going to do. I was going to be a script editor and a writer, and I have achieved all this. It was very sophisticated to drink wine and I thought I was terribly grown-up at 18.

'I began to enjoy drinking, to be on the kind of high that I am on every day now in a sober state (I am working now as a healer). In order to attain that high when I was younger, I had to drink more and more. Alcohol was enough to keep me happy; I never took any other drugs. It was the only way I could cope with my psychic side. I could see things that other people couldn't.

'From the age of about 20, drinking had become a regular thing. I always had a bottle of wine at dinner. By this time I was a script editor's secretary, and very much climbing up the ladder. I enjoyed the work.

'I was starting to get used to drinking. I didn't really drink a great deal then, but I drank consistently, seven days a week. It was only three glasses of wine, but so long as I had those three glasses I was all right. Drinking was a normal way of life and it never occurred to me that I was addicted to the stuff. But I would never go to a place where there wasn't any booze. I like going into museums and churches on holiday, but I would visit a church and find the nearest bar straight afterwards. I was very rarely drunk, but I was never sober.

'By the time I was 27 I had my first play on television. All this time, I was denying everything about myself, including a very strong spiritual side. If you were to say to me, "Are you a religious person?" I'd say "Of course not," and then go away and have the screaming abdabs all on my own. And drink some more.

'It's difficult to explain all this now that I've been living as a sober person for the last two-and-a-half years and life is a vivid, wonderful thing. I still have fantasies about drink now and again, especially when things get a little bit unsteady emotionally, or if I get depressed because I'm not earning money. But I know now that I've got far too much to lose by drinking, and that I'd kill myself very much quicker. The physical effects of alcohol would do that.

'Yes, I did try to give it up. I tried to give it up at one time every alternate Monday evening, when I had to catch the train north to work on a TV soap. It was a very punishing schedule. I was producing something like 100 pages every ten days and at the same time working on 30-page re-writes for six months. It was actually part and parcel of me cracking up.

'I was getting little signs of wanting to stop, but I couldn't. I remember one evening sitting in a pub waiting for someone and I was watching a woman who was drinking. Within a very short period of time – I don't mean this in a sexist way at all – she dissolved from an attractive 25-year-old blonde to a 50-year-old hag because she was getting drunk. Her face took on the look of somebody who has been through a stroke. She aged in front of me. I watched her, and I thought, "Is this going to happen to me?"

'Through all this time, I wasn't talking very much. I was going into these rages, internal rages which I couldn't express, and so I was drinking more and more. But it still didn't occur to me that I was hooked. I wasn't on a park bench. I wasn't underneath the arches at Charing Cross.

'All this time I was denying myself, my feelings, what was really there. I am a very emotional, spiritual, powerful person, and I was denying absolutely everything. I couldn't cope with having any influence over anybody, either, or with anyone coming up and saying nice things to me. I'd say, "Oh, they must have been drunk."

'I had been brought up to believe that the horrendous problems between my parents were all my fault, and I had an overwhelming sense of guilt. I was a constant people-pleaser, constantly seeking affection, but always doing it inappropriately. If you are never sober, you can't discriminate between people and situations anyway.

'I was mixing with people who drank even more than I did. It was as though I deliberately chose people who were even more excessive than I was. That made me feel all right.

'By October, 1984, I was showing signs of cracking up. The contract was finished and I had delivered all my scripts.

'I stayed at home and cried every day for six months. I couldn't leave this house; it was very difficult for me to answer the door. I couldn't go down the road to get a newspaper; it was like walking around with no skin on all the time.

'At this point I decided to try acupuncture. I felt that this might be the way to get well, and I first went in February 1985.

'After the first treatment I felt tired, depressed, and almost as though the needles were still in me for about 24 hours. But I kept going once a week. After about the fifth session, I stopped drinking. Gail, my acupuncturist (Directory: 153 Clapham High Street, London SW4), said that it was an extremely fast reaction. I knew I wasn't going to drink any more. I knew I was going forward, with the acupuncture, with the whole of myself, everything. Gail counselled me as much as she could.

'By about July I started to feel better and happier. Then I began to re-assess my life. I also went into therapy in June, and I had a lot of support from my friends (although to some extent I found I had to change my friends. The woman I live with was drinking, but recently she had started to cut down, so we have both changed). I also do Tai-Chi – I still do – and I meditate. My diet is good; I eat a wide range of foods and I sometimes take a few vitamins. The psychotherapy ended in about April 1986. I had to understand my background, the whole of my past life, and myself. I can get addicted to anything – people, places, things – even toothpaste.

'These experiences are all part and parcel of being a healer now and help me to understand. When I put the booze down I knew that I was going to be able to help people to heal themselves. I used to say, "Why am I psychic? I don't know. It doesn't matter anyway. Let's have another drink." Now I use it.

'I still have acupuncture, about once every two or three months. I enjoy it. It's a tuning-up process.

'I'm a living example of what it can do. I was in the worst possible state psychologically, at the bottom of the barrel, as well as being dependent on drink. Acupuncture has an effect on the brain, on everything. I would recommend it absolutely for anyone trying to give up alcohol.

'I can't just have a glass of wine because I would drink the whole bottle. So I have stopped it entirely. Sobriety is a wonderful state to be in. I was never sober before. The whole experience has changed me and changed my life.

'I have not drunk any alcohol since March 25, 1985.'

Some advice on giving up

AA, ACCEPT and Alcohol Concern are all extremely valuable in helping a heavy drinker to recover from his dependency. Drink-watchers help people who wish to cut down on their drinking rather than cut it out completely.

These organizations (please see Directory) offer a wide range of counselling, psychotherapy, and many other valuable activities, and help you to feel that you belong to a group where everyone understands your problem and where you do not feel alone or peculiar. Most alternative practitioners I interviewed said that they encourage their patients to attend one of these groups as well.

Look forward. Guilt about the past isn't going to do any good; it's now that matters. 'The emphasis here is not on past mistakes, but on the *here and now*.' (ACCEPT publication)

Decide whether you are going to cut down on your drinking or whether you need to stop completely. You may find it helpful to discuss this with your practitioner and any organization you go to for help, but in the end the decision is yours. Having done this, work out your own individual ways of achieving your goal. You are more likely to keep to the rules if you have set them up yourself.

You will need coping strategies to avoid alcohol. You may like to look at the new range of low-alcohol and non-alcoholic drinks (see chart). If you are heavily addicted to alcohol, it may not be wise for you to have even these, but discuss them with the people helping you and get expert advice. Organizations on alcohol dependency and drinking control take differing views.

Drinking less alcohol

Here is a list of drinks from which most of the alcohol has been removed. (Products labelled 'alcohol free' contain less than 0.05 per cent alcohol by volume. 'De-alcoholized' can be applied to products containing up to 0.5 per cent. 'Low alcohol' is legally meaningless.)

	Alcohol content	On sale in
Lagers		
Barbican alcohol-free	0.5%	
Birrell low-alcohol	1.0%	
Clausthaler low-alcohol	0.6%	Tesco
Kaliber alcohol-free	0.05%	Tesco
Panther low-alcohol	0.5%	
Sainsbury's low-alcohol	0.6%	Sainsbury's
St Christopher alcohol-free	0.05%	
Swan Special Light	0.9%	
Beers		
Highway low-alcohol ale	1%	
Shandy Barrel	less than 1.2%	
Wines		
Eisberg alcohol-free white	0.05%	Sainsbury's
Jung's de-alcoholized, red/white/rosé	0.5%	
Masson Light de-alcoholized	0.49%	Sainsbury's
Sainsbury's alcohol-free white	0.05%	Sainsbury's
Weisslack white	0.5%	Sainsbury's
White Wedding or No. 7 white	0.5%	
Wunderbar de-alcoholized white	0.5%	
Cider		
Low-alcohol cider (distributed by Leisure Drinks)	0.3%	
Coolers and cocktails		
Splitz (blend of fruit juice, carbonated water and wine)	10% wine	
Drivers' non-alcoholic drinks: gin and tonic whiskey american ginger white rum and cola	0.5%	
Others		
Jung's de-alcoholized vermouth	0.3%	

There is a new and expanding range of fruit juices, soft drinks and – currently the most fashionable – mineral waters on sale now. Many people choose these drinks rather than run the risk of a driving accident on the way home.

It will help to find new interests in life and new hobbies (and probably new friends) which do not involve drinking. You may end up altering your living habits quite drastically.

Some physical activity is good for you, as is relaxation; you may decide to learn a relaxation technique as well. ACCEPT include both exercise and relaxation classes in their programme.

A return to your old drinking habits is most likely when you are off-balance in some way. Avoid getting hungry, depressed, tired or upset if you possibly can. But don't go to pieces if you relapse. Lots of people have setbacks, so you won't be the only one. Pick yourself up again.

The family of a person with an alcohol problem is usually very worried about it. He or she may deny that there *is* a problem, and relatives can get angry, frustrated and afraid.

Al-Anon Family Groups offer help and counselling to the families and friends of problem drinkers.

Please see the directory for more information.

References

1 ACCEPT – Addictions Community Centres for Education, Prevention, Treatment and Research National HQ: 200 Seagrave Road, London SW6 1RQ Tel: 01 381 3155 Please also see information section.
2 *A Great and Growing Evil*, Royal College of Physicians, Tavistock Publications, 1987.
3 Aaron Neonberg et al, *Psychology Today*, January 1986.
4 H. Worning, *Clinical Gastroenterology* 13 (1984).
5 *Dictionary of Vitamins*, Leonard Mervyn Ph.D., Thorsons, 1984.
6 *Bestways*, USA, February, 1980.
7 J. B. Saunders et al, *Lancet*, 2 (1981).
8 H. A. Edmondson, *American Journal of Clinical Pathology*, 74 (1980).
9 The Endocrines and the Liver, *Serono Symposium* No. 51, M Langer et al, Academic Press, 1982.
10 *American Journal of Epidemiology* (1984). *Alternative Medicine Digest* (1985).
11 R. J. Sokol et al, *Alcoholism: Clinical and Experimental Research*
12 *Medicines: A guide for everybody*, Peter Parish (Penguin, 1983).
13 James S. Olms MD, *American Journal of Acupuncture*, 12 (1984)
14 Adam Lewenberg, *Clinical Therapeutics*, 7 (1985).
15 *Alcoholism: The Nutritional Approach*, Roger J. Williams Ph.D. (University of Texas Press, 1978).

16 *Diet, Crime and Delinquency*, Alexander Schauss (Parker House, 1981).
17 John P. Leary MD, *The American Chiropractor* (1985).
18 *Nutritional Medicine*, Dr Stephen Davies and Dr Alan Stewart (Pan Books, 1987).
19 Highland Psychiatric Research Group, Dr Iain Glen et al.
20 *Detox*, Dr Phyllis Saifer and M Zellerbach (Jeremy P. Tarcher, 1984).
21 *Amino Acids in Therapy*, Leon Chaitow (Thorsons, 1985).
22 M. Shafii MD et al, *American Journal of Psychiatry*, 123 (1975).

Caffeine

Coffee, tea and cola drinks contain caffeine (see chart). There are also significant amounts in chocolate and some drugs, particularly over-the-counter 'pep' pills and painkillers.

Caffeine in drinks

Brewed coffee	100 to 150 mg of caffeine per cup	
Instant coffee	86 to 99 mg	
Tea	60 to 75 mg	
Cola drinks	40 to 60 mg per can	
Decaffeinated coffee	2 to 4 mg per cup	

An intake of 250 mg and over a day is considered harmful.

Effects

In moderation, caffeine is very useful. A welcome cup of coffee makes us feel energetic and clear-headed. We associate tea and coffee with taking a break, watching the world go by. Putting the kettle on is the first thing many of us think of when we want to be hospitable. Most of us have the sense not to sip all day.

Coffee has plenty of niacin (vitamin B_3), trace amounts of other B vitamins and some minerals. Tea has plenty of the mineral manganese and trace amounts of other nutrients and, although it has less caffeine, it contains another stimulant, tannin.

However, caffeine is a stimulating, addictive drug, which acts on the central nervous system, especially the brain, and on muscles, the kidneys, the adrenal glands and the metabolic processes.

Coffee, high in caffeine, has several undesirable effects. It raises blood pressure, so in excess it should be avoided by those with hypertension. It increases heart rate and high doses can cause irregular heartbeat, and heavy coffee drinkers have been found to have a higher risk of heart disease.[1]

Because both coffee and tea stimulate the kidneys, they should be cut down or avoided by those with kidney problems, bladder irritation or prostatic enlargement. They can keep you awake at night and may cause night-time 'restless legs'.

Excess coffee and tea have many effects on digestion. They can reduce iron and zinc absorption and interfere with the digestion of protein. Caffeine increases the production of stomach acid, so it should be avoided by people with digestive troubles, including ulcers; some people find that coffee gives them heartburn by relaxing the lower end of the oesophagus (food pipe). The oils in coffee can irritate the gut and the tannin in tea causes constipation. Too much tea delays starch digestion. Both can cause a mild deficiency of Vitamin B_1, and both contain oxalic acid, which can damage the kidneys and encourage calcium loss. Too much coffee can cause a build-up of a toxic mineral, cadmium.

Coffee causes a slight rise in blood fats, but tea does not. In a Norwegian study, patients with high blood cholesterol levels who stopped drinking coffee for ten weeks found that their levels went down.[2] Caffeine dilates blood vessels in the skin so too much can make your face flushed and make an inflammatory skin condition worse. Those with glaucoma should avoid it because it affects the blood vessels in the eyes. There is also a possible link with bladder cancer.

Coffee is a common food allergen and can set off a migraine in susceptible people. In some research reported in Miami,[3] 22 per cent of arthritics were found to be allergic to coffee.

This is a 'masked allergy', where the person is allergic to a food he is also addicted to and it is probably very common in heavy tea and coffee drinkers. Caffeine causes an increase in blood sugar, which is answered by an insulin release to bring the blood sugar down again. However, this too-rapid descent leaves you feeling tired and longing for another cup; one reason for the addiction.

Pregnant women should limit their intake of caffeine. A study at Wayne University in the US found that babies born to mothers drinking even modest amounts of coffee – two to five cups a day – were more likely to be premature and have poor reflexes. In a statement in 1980, the American Food and Drug Administration postulated a link between too much caffeine and birth defects.

Another worrying link is that suspected between too much coffee and breast cancer. A recent study[4] found that women taking between 31 and 250 mg of caffeine a day – again, a modest intake – had a one-and-a-half times increased chance of getting non-malignant breast disease; this risk increased with the amount of coffee taken. Other research found that non-malignant breast disease could be helped by stopping caffeine.[5]

Excess caffeine is clearly harmful and caffeine intoxication is classified as an organic mental disorder by the American Psychiatric Association.[6] In spite of this, and the fact that high doses of caffeine produce an anxiety state, coffee and tea are available on tap in psychiatric hospitals. Dr Vicky Rippere, a pioneer in the study of food and psychological disorders, writes:[7]

> *On the basis of many years of clinical experience, I reckon that there is about a 95 per cent chance of a patient who is referred to me with an 'anxiety' type of disorder to be suffering from caffeinism. Patients referred for anxiety management training are routinely found, when I bother to ask them, to be consuming excessive amounts of caffeine.*

She finds that coffee can make schizophrenia worse, and that patients with agoraphobia often improve if they give up coffee and tea. American psychiatrist Dr Verner Stillner comments:[9]

> *Coffee drinking is socially learned behaviour. You drink it when you get up in the morning, and there's coffee at work too. People tend to overlook the fact that caffeine is a drug with behavioural consequences and not a perfectly benign agent.*

Dr Stillner rejects the idea that, because we all drink it, it must be all right.

So, when we need a temporary boost, coffee and tea are pleasant and useful stimulants, and they improve intellectual performance.[8] But people who are tense, competitive and irritable to start with, and who drink coffee (and to a lesser extent, tea) continuously, will simply get worse, and might even get sick.

Because so few doctors recognize a caffeine addiction, there are no drug treatments for it.

However, there is very probably a link between states of anxiety and tension and high coffee and tea consumption. Caroline K, an acupuncturist (Directory: Barbican, London EC2), is sure that there is:

> *I often find that patients who are insomniacs or on tranquillizers are heavy coffee drinkers and have simply never been told that it is a very strong stimulant as well as being very toxic. Quite a few people actually drink 10 or 20 cups a day, but they are never told to cut down. Coffee and, to a lesser extent, tea are implicated in so many addictions, as an additional drug. People don't realize they are swinging about between uppers and downers – they use the coffee to get them going, and the tranquillizers to calm them down!*

A teacher of TM, Roger L (Directory: Nationwide) told me:

> *If you had asked for coffee during this interview, you wouldn't have got it! I remember teaching one lady to meditate, and she complained of palpitations during her meditation. She was obviously meditating correctly, but I questioned her and it turned out that every morning she had a large mug of Turkish coffee. I always say don't have any tea or coffee before meditating. What she was experiencing was the effect of the coffee; it had always been there, but she had been so busy rushing around before that she hadn't noticed it. It was quite a shock to her to discover the effect it had.*

Dr L (Directory: Upper Harley Street, London NW1) is one of those doctors aware of caffeinism.

> *A very common addiction. Although food addictions are easier to deal with because they don't have the negative connotations of many addictions, that is, they're not frowned upon, coffee is a strong social habit. All the same, many of my patients feel much less aggressive and less hyped up, when they are off coffee.*

Alternative practitioners and caffeinism

Caffeine addiction is usually part of the whole symptom picture. People do not usually realize that they would feel better if they cut it down, so practititioners include caffeine reduction as part of their whole approach.

Acupuncturist Evonne F (Directory: Victoria Road, London NW6) says:

> *People who are manic coffee drinkers, usually have a fractionally weak heart and circulation; in other words they need that boost. The energy needed to function at top speed during the day is lacking. If people get a good night's sleep, have a reasonable diet, and with the normal stress level that everyone is living under anyway, there shouldn't be the need for ten cups of coffee.*
>
> *Usually, if you take the coffee away, the whole system sags, the energy disappears. Then you see the true picture, which you can then treat. The moment you boost the body systems and organs which are least efficient right up to as near 100 per cent as you can get them, all desire for stimulants will disappear. The need to be boosted will not be there any more.*

Acupuncturist Caroline K encourages her patients to try caffeine-free drinks – Barleycup and all the herbal teas; but says:

> *People are very scared of changing from something like coffee; they feel that tea and coffee are an essential part of their lives. So I tell them – 'If you've got to have it, then take one or two cups a day as a treat, at the most.' In a way, I think if you are enjoying it that much occasionally, this slightly dampens out the bad effects it has on you. Tea is not as strong as coffee, not so toxic; but certainly if people are drinking more than four or five cups a day, I will tell them to cut down. I don't think people should be too hard on themselves.*

Another acupuncturist, Richard U (Directory: Wilbury Road, Hove, Sussex), stresses:

> *A lot of people use coffee because their adrenals are rather flagged. I think it's a lot to do also with fatigue and low blood sugar. I try to wean people off too much of it, and I give advice on nutrition too.*

Medical herbalist Julian B (Directory: Wilbury Road, Hove, Sussex) agrees that caffeine, although an antidote to fatigue, ends up making you feel more exhausted than ever.

> *I had a lady who came in with extreme fatigue. She couldn't understand why, even though she was drinking three-and-a-half litres of black coffee a day. It goes with a lifestyle, it's a poetic kind of relaxation. But she, like most coffee addicts, didn't believe she was addicted at all.*

Naturopath Norman E (Directory: Gatley Road, Cheadle, Cheshire) wrote to me:

> *Coffee is a great addiction. It is standard that some patients drink a cup of coffee first thing in the morning and again at 11 a.m. As the years roll by, the 11 a.m. becomes 10.30 a.m. and eventually 10 a.m. Then, more coffee. By then the adrenals are so out of tune that it is difficult for them to work correctly. So a very careful analysis has to be done, and it is not simply a question of giving the patient a remedy for the adrenals, but it may be that they have to have a detoxifying programme for the liver, too.*

Dr J (Directory: High Road, London N17) gave up a lot of coffee himself, and is sympathetic:

> *Most people don't come and ask me to stop them drinking coffee, but I do realize that it really grips some of us. It can be very difficult indeed to stop; it's a social thing, that's what makes it so hard to give up. But I do see giving up as part of my treatment for people. I offer them substitutes – coffee substitutes or herbal teas. The whole thing is an important ritual and I realize it's a change in the habits of the palate to change from coffee to these drinks. If you have had a hard morning's shopping and you really want a rest, you're not allowed into the café unless you buy something; so you can either buy additive-laden orange juice or caffeine-laced tea or coffee . . .*

Because caffeine over-stresses the central nervous system, nutritional support can help. Dr William H. Philpott, Director of the Philpott Medical Center in Oklahoma City, uses vitamins C, B_3, B_5, and B_6, with calcium and magnesium (both minerals which nourish the nerves), for all addictions, including caffeine.

A case history: Jane

Jane, like most other people, did not realize that her coffee consumption was giving her health problems.

'I was an enthusiastic coffee drinker. And I had had breast pains for several years. In spite of trying evening primrose oil, which was pretty good, the pains kept coming back, but my doctor couldn't find anything and so I made light of it.

'Then I read somewhere that there's a connection between breast disease and coffee, so I tried to stop. I was surprised to find it very hard; I got very tired and headachy. I felt a bit weepy too. I really needed my coffee to give me a boost.

'Anyway, I went to an acupuncturist – not for the coffee, but for the breast pains, which were still nagging me a bit. He gave me electro-acupuncture, without needles. He also gave me some homoeopathic pills to take. After several treatments, I felt the breast pains disappearing. But the odd thing was that my desire for coffee was getting less as well. I got so I was drinking it more out of habit than need, so I gradually cut it down. Now, I just have a couple of cups every week; it's in the nature of a treat for me now. My practitioner told me that, as my energy levels came back, my need for coffee would diminish. And he agreed, incidentally, that it could cause breast troubles.

'Decaffeinated coffee gives me indigestion, but I enjoy herbal teas, weak china tea and fruit juices and mineral water are particularly refreshing and good. I really do feel more energetic and stable now.'

Altering the ritual: substitutes for coffee and tea

If you drink a lot of coffee or tea and you stop all at once, you may feel tired, headachy and rather touchy. So you may prefer to cut down gradually.

Simply drinking your tea and coffee weaker is a good first step. Some people find that diluting ordinary coffee with decaffeinated works quite well, too, and there is also tea available with less caffeine in it. However, decaffeinated coffee is a mixed blessing. Although it contains very little caffeine (see chart on p. 45) it stimulates acid stomach secretions and can cause indigestion. If you find that it suits you, please bear in mind that the best kinds are probably those made using a water process of carbon dioxide to remove the caffeine. Café Hag, Nairobi Pure Kenya, decaffeinated Nescafé and Sainsbury's decaffeinated Gold Choice are made in this way. Some decaffeinated coffees are processed using chemical solvents (usually methyl chloride, ethylene acetate or dichloromethane). Methyl chloride is suspected by the US National Institute of Environmental Sciences to be, in vast doses, a carcinogen.[10]

The least harmful time to drink coffee and tea is about 4 p.m. They will perk you up and do less damage to your nerves then. Another tip is that tea bags release less caffeine than tea brewed from leaves. Coffee substitutes – Barleycup, Bamboo and dandelion coffee – and herbal teas are very popular now and there is a wide range on sale at your local health food store. Occasionally you might enjoy some fresh fruit or vegetable juice, or the latest rising trend, bottled mineral water.

Coffee and tea are a pleasant social ritual. So, whether you decide to cut down or cut out, don't deny yourself. Just try to replace one welcome, habitual drink with another less harmful to your nerves and general health. Remember – no one's asking you to do without that valued break.

Please see the Directory for more information.

References

1 *Here's Health*, February 1986.
2 *Journal of Alternative Medicine*, November 1985.
3 *Twelfth Advanced Seminar in Clinical Ecology* 20 November, 1978.
4 C. Boyle et al, *Journal of the National Cancer Institute*, vol 72: 5.
5 V. Ernester et al, *Surgery* 1982, 91: 263.
6 *Third American Psychiatric Association's Diagnostic and Statistical Manual of Mental Disorders*, 1980.
7 *Society of Environmental Therapy Newsletter*, September 1984.
8 *Society of Enviromental Therapy Newsletter*, June 1985.
9 Interviewed in *Prevention* magazine, vol 22: 10.
10 *Here's Health*, October 1982.

Cocaine

'Now, it's cocaine. Heroin among the bright young things is slightly passé.' (A practitioner)

Cocaine is a white crystalline powder, originally from the leaves of the coca bush, which grows mainly in Peru and Bolivia. South American Indians have chewed coca leaves to reduce tiredness and suppress hunger since at least 2,500 BC, and it was also used in early times as a local anaesthetic.

During the Inca Empire period from the 13th to the 16th century, coca was declared the gift of the sun god and called the 'Divine Plant'. Its ability to stimulate breathing and heart rate was useful to the Incas, many of whom lived at a high altitude where the air is thin.

When the Catholic Spaniards first conquered South America in the 16th century, they were at first shocked by the use of cocaine, which they condemned as part of the natives' ungodly rituals. But when they saw the difference it made to their slaves, who could work in the gold and silver mines and on the plantations for longer hours and less food, they changed their minds and instead put a tax on it, thus bringing in revenues for the church.

By the mid-19th century the active principle had been isolated from the coca plant and cocaine was part of orthodox medicine. Under its influence, Robert Louis Stevenson wrote *The Strange Case of Dr Jekyll and Mr Hyde* in six days. Sigmund Freud tried it and found it a marvellous drug, giving euphoria and energy. In 1884 he published a paper, *On Coca*, praising its effects and recommending it for opiate and alcohol addicts. But even then doctors were becoming aware of its dangers and his paper provoked heated objections. He gave cocaine to a friend, Ernst von Fleischl, who was trying to give up morphine, but von Fleischl then became addicted to cocaine and remained so until his death. Freud eventually changed his mind about cocaine, but in his autobiography he does not mention the controversy at all.

Meanwhile, cocaine in patent medicines was tremendously popular, being used for anything from syphilis to sore nipples. One American concoction, Ryno's Hay Fever-'n'-Catarrh Remedy, was almost pure cocaine. It was put into tonic wines, too; one cocaine and wine mixture, Vin Mariani, was Pope Leo XIII's favourite. Coca Cola appeared in 1885, but it only ever contained very small amounts and these were taken out in 1903.

Sherlock Holmes used cocaine to give him the obsessive, intense energy for solving a case. But as public opinion swung against it, Conan Doyle changed the tone of his stories and Dr Watson's disapproval intensified. By 1896, in *The Missing Three Quarters*, Doyle was hinting that the great detective's obsession with his arch-enemy, Moriarty, was paranoic and the result of cocaine.

During the First World War, prostitutes sold cocaine to British troops on leave in London. The press reacted by saying that this was a German plot to destroy the British Empire, and regulations were passed restricting its use to medical professionals. After years of being less popular (although it was part of the plot in Dorothy L. Sayers' *Murder Must Advertise*) it surfaced again in America during the 1960s, where it was known as 'the champagne drug'.

Easily smuggled into the USA, it is widely used now by American socialites, rock singers, sportsmen – those people who need to feel good all the time and for whom feeling confident and energetic is a necessary part of their image. Dr Richard Miller, of the American clinic Cokenders, estimates that there are over 2.2 million American addicts and deaths are put at over 1,000 a year.

Although drug agencies formerly thought that cocaine was too expensive to catch on in the UK, its use is spreading. (Nevertheless, very few people yet ask for help for primary cocaine addiction.) The current price is £50 to £70 a gram; a new user might take a quarter of a gram over a weekend and a habitual user one or two grams a day.

Although cocaine (except as a local anaesthetic) can legally be supplied now only under a special licence, it is the fastest-growing drug of abuse here. In June 1987 a cache of over 50 kilos was seized in London.

In fact, cocaine is a world problem. The World Health Organization (WHO) estimates that there are about 750,000 heroin addicts worldwide. The figure for cocaine addiction is 4.8 million.

Effects

Sniffed up the nostrils or injected, cocaine kicks the central nervous system into an immediate reaction. Stress hormones are released, and blood pressure, heart and breathing rate and body temperature rise. It brings strong feelings of confidence, optimism and assertiveness. During a high-dosage 'spree', the user can't get his words out fast enough, can't breathe properly or sit still. After the initial 'high' lasting about an hour, however, depression follows, with bad temper and extreme pessimism. Some users try to avoid the letdown by taking other drugs, even heroin, and a combination can be extremely toxic. WHO says that smoking rather than sniffing cocaine is more dangerous because the action is more rapid and it is harder to control the dosage. Dirty needles can cause tetanus, hepatitis, inflammation of the heart, abscesses, cellulitis and infections at the injection site.

Long-term use damages the brain, lungs and liver and can cause anorexia. It can precipitate irregular heartbeat, with the increased risk of heart attack, stroke and embolism. The liver can regenerate itself, but the heart cannot. There may be cold sweats, tremors and teeth-grinding. When snorted up the nose, cocaine can cause irritated nose and throat membranes, nosebleeds, blocked sinuses and decreased resistance to colds and 'flu. Years of heavy use erode the nasal septum separating the nostrils, leaving a hole. Addicts may suffer nausea, insomnia and over-excitablity, with feelings of disorientation, and exhaustion and muscle pains. High dosage may bring a mystic feeling of near-completeness, but the addict may become paranoic, with feelings of great anxiety and a fear of going mad. It can cause distorted perceptions, even hallucinations, and the addict may think that 'coke bugs' are crawling all over his skin and be completely overwhelmed by a nameless terror. Eventually, there may be loss of control over basic bodily functions, with exaggerated reflexes, failure to respond to stimuli, and coma, seizures and even brain damage. Death may result from breathing cessation or a heart attack.

Freebasing and crack

These ways of taking cocaine to get an even greater high are less common at the moment in Britain.

Freebasing is when a street mixture – usually cocaine hydrochloride salt – is cooked, dried, and injected or inhaled. The effect is instantaneous, and a single dose can cause seizures, fainting and convulsions. Some people get toxic psychosis, with hallucinations, paranoia and extreme aggression. It can cause permanent damage to the mouth, throat and lungs.

Crack is cocaine mixed with baking powder and water to make pellets which are then smoked in pipes. It gives a huge boost to the blood pressure in seconds and can be lethal. Its effects last a shorter time so it is more addictive than ordinary cocaine and overdosing is more common because the dose is difficult to control.

Both these ways of taking cocaine are extremely dangerous, and can be lethal.

Although it is generally believed that cocaine creates psychological, rather than physical dependence, researchers at Concordia University, Montreal, state that the drug 'produces a more tenacious dependency than heroin.'[1] and laboratory monkeys, when addicted, will choose cocaine over food and sex until they die.

Withdrawals

Although a cocaine dependency is thought at present to be mostly psychological, the symptoms of withdrawal involve both mind and body, producing severe fatigue, anxiety and depression, with hunger, nausea, chills and tremors, and strong cravings for the drug. Heavy users can experience muscle aches and twitches, insomnia, an itching nose, with occasionally delusions and hallucinations. These withdrawals usually go away within a week.

The main problem with stopping cocaine is that it gives the user so much confidence that he thinks he can give it up at any time, and will not admit to his addiction. For this reason, some experts think it can be harder to come off cocaine than to come off heroin.

Drug treatments for cocaine addiction

No definitive drug treatment has yet emerged for cocaine, but a few drugs have been tried, on a small scale.[2]

Cocaine can make you feel:

- Agitated and psychotic
- Depressed afterwards.

Drug treatments focus on stopping these extreme reactions.

Diazepam (Valium), sometimes with propranolol (propranolol hydrochloride – Inderal), has been used to calm people down, and the major tranquillizer, chlorpromazine (Taractan) and lithium (lithium carbonate, lithium sulphate – Camcolit, Liskonum, Phasal, Priadel) have a stabilizing effect.

Methylphenidate (methylphenidate hydrochloride – Ritalin) produces euphoria and has been given for the post-cocaine 'crash'.

All these drugs have unpleasant and sometimes dangerous side-effects.

The amino acids tyrosine and tryptophan have also been tried, with a drug. (Amino acids, the building blocks of protein, are currently being researched for their therapeutic value. Used correctly, they are non-toxic.)

Drugless treatments for cocaine addiction

Acupuncture

Evonne F (Directory: Victoria Road, London NW6) has treated several users.

With a cocaine addict, you get a particular type of personality. They are usually party jokers, who are laughing all the time about everything. You feel as if everything is tongue-in-cheek; there is inappropriate laughter, or a total lack of laughter; the sad clown, theatrical. A lot of actors and actresses have that syndrome. They need that energy boost, that joy which they don't naturally have, that laughter which perhaps isn't really there. Very often you see them in social surroundings, being the life and soul of the party, but if you go home with them there's very often no communication, no joy. In fact, there's depression.

Cocaine boosts your heart, your enthusiasm, your fire. As the heart starts beating faster it influences the kidneys and the bladder which, along an acupuncture pathway, supply energy to the heart. So, after even a few days on cocaine, sometimes, you get tremendous low back pain; the kidneys are being overworked.

Ron K also used acupuncture on a young addict (Directory: Neal's Yard, London WC2), together with cranial osteopathy (discussed later).

Cocaine particularly depletes the kidneys so it's very important to treat the kidney point; also, the adrenals get exhausted. Cocaine affects the heart indirectly, via stimulation of the sympathetic nervous system. But I treat the whole person every time as well.

Transcendental meditation

Roger L, a teacher of Transcendental Meditation (Directory: Nationwide), feels that cocaine gives a phoney, artificial 'high' which counterbalances the user's fatigue and depression, but that people who meditate grow out of this need.

People are taking it to get effects. But the natural benefits of TM are such that people aren't going to want to get those highs, which are such an enormous strain on the physiology and psychology. The clarity that comes with meditation, the well-being, the energy – these are based on the relief of stress and the refinement of the nervous system. You don't get withdrawl symptoms with meditation. You don't come down from meditation; it's balanced, progressive.

So, when people start to learn, they generally want to come off their drugs, because they realize that it's not worth doing. In any case, there is anxiety often associated with taking drugs. People feel good, but inside there's an uneasiness about it; a restlessness.

I remember that with the Big Bang in the City, a lot of people started taking cocaine to help them cope with the strain. What's also interesting is that we are getting more and more people from the City learning to meditate. They are discovering that there's a different way of functioning that doesn't require either having a heart attack or a stroke when you get to 40, or taking drugs to keep going, either. They find things a lot easier. They're much happier.

Cranial osteopathy

Ron K says:

I treated a young man who had been addicted for two years. Heavy dosage. He blew £70,000 on it.

He was a TV actor. He was thrown into stardom, went to the States and had an emotional upset; a relationship broke up. He went to pieces, went on the cocaine.

I did an assessment from several different angles. One is taking the pulses, part of traditional Chinese acupuncture (please see acupuncture, same practitioner). I was able to classify the emotional picture. I also did cranial manipulation. The bones of the skull move slightly, and with all the cases I have seen of cocaine addiction there is a flexion lesion on the occiput, a lack of proper flexibility. The cranial approach is to loosen up and bring harmony to the cranium, so that all the components are rhythmically moving very slightly as they should.

Treatment is an ongoing process; by releasing the cranium, a lot of emotional release takes place too. It's like peeling an onion; little by little, you find that layers of the being come to light. A patient will re-live some of the pain that the drug was insulating him or her from. So during the treatment, it's important to be supportive; they can go down a bit.

I didn't talk to him about coming off. I let two weeks go by with treatments, without discussing with him how much he was taking or how he could pull out. Then, when I thought the time was ripe, I said, 'How about trying a week without it?' I made him promise to himself and to me not to touch it for that week. He had friends supporting him, but he had to be careful because some were users. So he had to insulate himself a bit from part of his social environment.

I had a couple of 'phone calls from him while he was going through it. He was rather depressed, and said, 'What's the point of all this? I feel like going out and finding some coke.' But he didn't. I also gave him a vitamin complex, and a diet.

Just having acupuncture and cranial treatment slows you down quite a bit, so I didn't give him any additional relaxation. But I did persuade him to start playing tennis again. Coming off for him was very quick – just a few weeks.

Cocaine insulates you by making you feel good, just as tranquillizers can insulate you, but in a different way. Unlike heroin addiction, where there is a much bigger physical reaction, in cocaine there isn't that kind of reaction. It's much more a pyschological craving.

American osteopaths Darryl Espeland and Christian Peters have written about the treatment of addiction with both osteopathy and cranial osteopathy. They find that drug-free therapies can relieve stress and anxiety and encourage trust between practitioner and patient, as treatment works to correct the emotional and physical imbalance accompanying addiction. They find that substance abusers are physically and emotionally out of balance and that the physician's own energy during the manipulative techniques can re-establish the balance.[3]

A case history: Peter

'I first came across it when I was about 17. I am now 27 and am a bond dealer in the City of London. I never really took it much when I was young; it was too expensive, and it didn't appeal to me.

'By the age of 24 I knew some people who were using an awful lot of coke and I tried it again; I snorted it. You cut a line of coke out on a hard surface with a razor blade, chop the stuff up, draw it into a line and then sniff it up with a straw. It takes a minute or so to work.

'It's a great feeling, a very, very nice feeling. You feel very strong, powerful, very together, very clear mentally – or you think you are. You can do anything; you're on top of the world. And it's not only in the mind, it's physically a good feeling too.

'People say it's not addictive, but you are always trying to get that feeling back, that fantastic high. If you start by just having a couple of lines at the beginning of the evening, after about half an hour or so it's wearing off again and the temptation is that as you're coming down you just want a little more, to perk you up again.

'I was doing quite a lot, on and off. It didn't cost much to start with; I had friends who used to give it to me quite a bit. It was readily available at parties; people always seemed to have a supply with them. At nightclubs, we'd go to the men's room and take it. It was frighteningly common. Friends would have little envelopes, little stashes with them.

'When you're feeling together and energetic, you feel you can dance the night away. The down afterwards wasn't a huge depressing down. I understand that with freebasing you get a much worse down. Usually late at night, when you're wrecked anyway, you get the down.

'At one time I was taking at least 5 grams a week. I used to pay about £60 or £70 a gram. Dealers were – and are – very easy to find, and in some restaurants the waiters have it.

'Then I started getting very tired during the day, and I was using it at work occasionally to keep me going. My work suffered appallingly. It temporarily clears the head, but you have to go on using it. It doesn't work in the long run. After a lot of coke I would get palpitations, but by then it didn't worry me; you feel so wonderful, you don't think there can be anything wrong with you.

'I never considered myself an addict, not even later, when I was taking much more. Not for a moment. You don't.

'I got to the stage where I was doing it quite a lot and very regularly. My health was suffering terribly. I was very tired, very run down, getting maybe four hours' sleep a night. I got a lot of colds and I was consistently very, very depressed. Then I was particularly ill and I was eventually admitted to hospital. My body's defence systems had just packed up. I was in an isolation ward. Everyone wore masks; they weren't sure what was the matter with me. This really scared me an awful lot.

'At that point I realized that I was damaging myself, that I had to take control over my life. I decided then and there to stop dead. Being in hospital stopped me anyway from getting any coke. I was very ill and I couldn't tell if I had any withdrawals.

'I took a holiday and came back feeling better and went back to work; still the same work, as a bond dealer. Other people in the office were taking coke. It was – and is – just so common in the City. And I was still using it, on and off, if it was there. I always felt wrecked, had slight nosebleeds after it and it still made me very tired. It was still a temptation; I hadn't really given up.

'I started Transcendental Meditation purely by chance. I went to a TM meeting after meeting someone, stayed, and decided to learn. But I didn't learn TM to get off coke.

'I started to do 20 minutes' TM in the morning and 20 minutes in the evening. Basically, mentally and physically everything comes to an equilibrium. It takes you to a very peaceful state and lets everything balance itself. TM showed me that I didn't need coke, that there was enough going on inside me, and that I didn't need the outside stimulus of coke or anything else. It got to the point where I wasn't interested in taking it any more.

'It wasn't a sudden revelation, though. It happened gradually.

I couldn't say this was a wonder cure. The decision has to come from within you first; the TM just helps you to realize inside that you don't really want the drug. It's much nicer getting high doing TM than getting high on cocaine because it's completely natural. You realize how powerful your body is, and you can get yourself into any state you want. You have total control over yourself.

'I have been doing TM for about ten months now. I had my last coke a few weeks before I started TM, at a party just before Christmas, 1986. There was somebody there with a couple of grams on them. I knew I shouldn't be doing it, and that it was wrecking me, but I just wanted it. You have to have it, you can't say no. It's a mental craving.

'Now, I've seen it used in front of me and I don't have any craving or wish to use it. TM has changed everything, turned everything around.

'TM has had other effects. I have become more productive and efficient at work and my salary has increased. I'm much less frenetic than I was. Working in the City, you build up a lot of stress. The 'phones are going, you're on two or three lines, screaming, and you do feel terribly tense and worn down. But since I have been doing TM I find I can take three calls at once when the 'phones are ringing like crazy.

'It's so simple to learn and do. It takes so little out of the day and adds so much. I would recommend TM to anyone who is addicted and who has made the decision to give up. A lot of my friends are surprised at the change in me and several are learning now. It's catching; it's going round.

'Cocaine is acceptable. It's not thought to be addictive, but simply a safe, recreational drug. It gets a good press as well; all the people seen to be taking it are actors, actresses, people in the public eye, which makes it very glamorous. It's frighteningly easy to get hold of too.

'Everyone's your friend once you have a gram on you. But as soon as you've finished your packet, they'll be off after someone else. The sheer desperation of people trying to get a line off somebody is very frightening; they have to have it. It's sick, very sick.

'You say to yourself, "I'm not an addict, I'm not an addict", but you know damned well that if there's some there you can't say no to it.'

Please see the directory for more information.

References

1 *The Times*, 14 July 1986.
2 H. K. Kleber and F. Gawin, *Journal of Clinical Psychiatry*, 2 December, 1984,
3 *Osteopathic Annals*, vol 13, February 1985.

Heroin

'Heroin, I love you. You are God, heroin; without you, I am nothing.'
(An addict)

Heroin is a white crystalline powder. It belongs to the same family of narcotics as morphine, codeine and methadone, all opioids derived from or related to the opium poppy. It is a major mind-altering and addictive drug.

The secrets of the white opium poppy were known to the ancient Greeks, Arabs and Egyptians, and guarded by a select few who understood its power. Opium use eventually spread across Asia Minor to India and the Far East until, by the early 1880s, it was established in Europe. It was widely used by the Victorians in laudanum and, at the turn of this century, Sir William Osler described opium as 'God's own medicine'.

The word 'heroin' was coined by Heinrich Dreser, a pharmacist, and in 1898 the drug was synthesized. The German firm Bayer were the first to market it – as a cough suppressant. In 1968 it was banned without prescription under the Misuse of Drugs Act.

Now, heroin worth over £100 million a year is flooding the UK market (although there has been a slight drop recently in favour of cocaine). In 1985, 8,819 addicts – mostly heroin – were notified to the Home Office. But a survey published in the British Medical Journal and quoted in *The Times* on 15 August 1986, suggests a total of about 40,000 *new cases* of heroin addiction every year. Even allowing for differences in definition and under-notification by doctors, the Home Office figures are obviously a huge under-estimate.

Heroin now is easy to get and – to begin with – cheap. As D

David Owen said recently, 'The cost of keeping high on drugs over the weekend is lower than the cost of getting smashed in a pub', and it's true that, for a new user, an effective fix only costs about £5. But, when tolerance comes and the user needs more and more, he or she must spend several hundred pounds a week on the habit.

Users are mostly young, between 18 and 30, and they get their first fix from friends, perhaps drawn to experiment with heroin by its powerful mythology. Abuse is mainly in the North of England where there is high unemployment and poverty and, although heroin is not addictive to start with, about 90 per cent of those who try it will get hooked.

Effects

Heroin now is less often injected and more likely to be sniffed or smoked. Injecting is more dangerous, especially when dirty needles are used; AIDS can spread easily this way (which is why disposable needles are being given to addicts) and infections can cause abscesses, hepatitis, tetanus and endocarditis (inflamation of the heart). Injecting can also cause almost instant dependence. 'Chasing the dragon' means the commoner method of inhaling the fumes given off when powdered heroin is melted over heated tinfoil.

Street heroin is often mixed with other powders to make it go further, and this adulterated version can cause kidney failure. Several addicts in the US, Amsterdam and Paris have been blinded by yeast spores of candida albicans in Middle East heroin.

With the first dose, heroin gives a euphoric 'rush'. This fades, to be followed by drowsiness ('the nod'), clouded thoughts, and a lack of anxiety and appetite. This effect lasts for between six and twelve hours. Heroin does this by depressing all body systems, including the central nervous system, thus slowing heart rate, breathing and bowel function. Blood vessels are dilated and you feel warm and relaxed, and mental and physical pain are blotted out. This is why it has been such a useful medical drug.

In time, heroin changes the workings of every body cell. Its continued use causes constipation, sickness and muscle wasting. Other effects over time are nausea and vomiting, dizziness, malnutrition with anaemia and anorexia, and lowered resistance to infections. All opioid drugs suppress the production of male hormones, so men have a diminished sexual capacity. Women on heroin often don't bother with birth control and can produce addicted babies.

Overdose can cause lethargy and stupor; blood pressure drops, muscles relax and body temperature is low. Breathing slows and can even stop, killing the user.

After someone has been taking heroin for some time, he will have to take stronger and stronger doses just to satisfy the craving and ward off the dreaded withdrawals. When a person says, correctly, that he needs the drug in order to feel normal, he is an addict. Then, getting the next fix and the money to pay for it become an obsession, the only thing to think about and do. Nearly all addicts lie and steal for their habit. Being a heroin addict is a lifestyle, which includes membership of a society of outcasts.

Withdrawals

The brain produces its own chemicals – endorphins – for enhancing pleasure and reducing pain. The action of heroin and other narcotics is to replace these natural chemicals so that, eventually, the brain is left without either the support of the drug or its own endorphins. The deprived, unbalanced nervous system starts putting out confused messages and these are the symptoms of withdrawal.

Severity of the symptoms depends on the degree of drug dependence – how long it has been taken, and how much – and on the body's ability to adapt to doing without the drug and begin working naturally again.

Withdrawals begin when the addict needs another fix. They usually start with watery eyes and a running nose, cold sweats, restlessness, yawning and intermittent sleep; rather like a bad dose of 'flu. Later, he may find he cannot keep still or find a comfortable position; he feels shaky, extremely irritable and anxious, with intense cravings for the drug. This can turn into lethargy, weakness and depression, with nausea, vomiting and diarrhoea, chills and stomach cramps, insomnia, and pains in the back and legs with spasmodic kicking movements. The skin is cold and covered with gooseflesh, which is where the term 'cold turkey' comes from. After 72 to 96 hours, these symptoms start to abate and are usually over in about two weeks.

But there may also be later, secondary, withdrawal symptoms; minor disturbances in body temperature and blood pressure, with depression or emotional instability and more cravings. It can take months for the body to resume normal physiological functioning. Painful feelings and conflicts, repressed by the heroin, may surface again and have to be dealt with.

Heroin is not the worst drug to withdraw from (among the worst are the benzodiazepine tranquillizers). In their report, *Young People and Heroin*,[1] published by the Health Education Council in November 1985, researchers state that fears of heroin are overplayed; the drug is not instantly addictive and coming off, although highly unpleasant, will not kill you. A director of the Society of Biophysical Medicine (Directory: Water Street, Liverpool) confirms this:

> *People can die from overdosing, and from mixing heroin with other drugs – there are all sorts of cocktails – and from dirty injections. But more people die from smoking and alcohol than heroin.*

Part of the drug's attraction, however, is 'a demonic mythology of heroin misuse, or the highly self-dramatized accounts of wealthy pop stars who trade in the romantic image of being taken to hell and back.'[1]

Many long-term users feel like passive victims, especially if they are unemployed as well. The drug flattens their emotions, deadening them against initiative and responsibility. They have to grow out of these attitudes if they are to grow out of the addiction. The network of friends and activities all wrapped around getting and using the drug must be left behind. One addict said that, when you give up, 'you have to sort of start your life again, put a lot behind you.'[1] And, as another said, 'abstinence is a fragile vessel.' It's not coming off that's so difficult. It's staying off.

Drug treatments for heroin addiction

A drug used to minimize heroin withdrawal is methadone (methadone hydrochloride or Physeptone), which acts over a longer period. Methadone seems to have only one advantage: it can wean the addict off street heroin, which can be dangerously contaminated. It is, however, just as addictive as heroin.

In spite of DHSS guidelines in 1984, warning doctors against prescribing methadone as a long-term treatment, the HEC report[1] states that it is still commonly given to heroin addicts.

In her book, *Hooked*,[2] Scottish surgeon Meg Patterson quotes from a *Lancet* report; methadone addicts suffer from fatigue, weakness, loss of weight and anorexia, depression and digestive disturbances often persisting long after treatment, which usually doesn't work anyway. It can take several months – some say longer than with heroin – for the methadone addict to return to normal health after giving up the drug. And American figures show that, ten years after treatment, less than ten per cent of those treated for either heroin or methadone addiction are still drug-free.

Dr Patterson writes, 'cigarettes are a harder addiction than heroin to stop, but methadone is the hardest of all to discontinue.'

Other drugs sometimes given to ease the first few days of withdrawal are clonidine (clonidine hydrochloride – Catapres, Dixarit) and buprenorphine (Temgesic).

Possible side-effects of clonidine are dry mouth, drowsiness, constipation, initial slowing of heart rate, and it may produce impotence, itching, swelling of the throat and face, nausea and dizziness.[3] Its abrupt withdrawal is often followed by anxiety, sweating, tremors and sometimes high blood pressure, and it may also be addictive.

Buprenorphine is probably addictive too. A letter in the *British Medical Journal*[4] describes using it to get a patient off alcohol and Diconal and concludes that 'the end result of a harrowing story is that he is now firmly addicted to buprenorphine and our attempts to wean him off it have so far been unsuccessful.'

A different approach is to give the addict a drug which, if he takes any heroin as well, will produce highly unpleasant effects. This is the purpose of naltrexone (injectable version naloxone, naloxone hydrochloride, Narcan). However, according to Dr Cushman, Professor of Pharmacology at Wisconsin University, addicts do not usually stick to their naltrexone, and many relapse back to heroin again after stopping it. Studies show that naltrexone is relatively useless, and that the proportion of patients still being treated after a regime over nine months is the same as in those not taking it. In addition, long-term use may damage the brain's ability to produce its own essential chemicals, the endorphins.

Although research into other chemical solutions continues,

the most important thing about the current drugs which are given to stop addictions to other drugs is that they seldom work. They often simply leave the unhappy addict with a different addiction. Since these drugs can also be extremely harmful, they cannot, by any stretch of the imagination, be said to 'detoxify'.

Drugless treatments for heroin addiction

Acupuncture

This is the foremost approach. I spoke to Ian W, a director of the Society of Biophysical Medicine, which uses electro-acupuncture.

Since the late 1970s we have had a lot of experience with treating Valium and Ativan addiction with acupuncture. Some of us also had previous experience of treating heroin addiction on a small scale. We were very impressed with the results, to such an extent that when the heroin problem started to surface on a very large scale we thought acupuncture might be a suitable treatment. Because one of the effects of acupuncture is to greatly reduce the severity of withdrawal symptoms, it is enabling the addicts to progressively cut back on their drug intake.

An addict is dependent upon heroin for a feeling of well-being; his brain has given up producing its own positive hormones, the endorphins. So, when he comes off the drug, his confused and distressed nervous system reacts, causing him acute misery. Acupuncture coaxes the brain into producing endorphins once more.

Work at St Bartholomew's Hospital found that concentrations of some endorphins in addicts who were withdrawing were raised by acupuncture,[5] and these results were repeated in research published in America among 119 addicts.[6] Dr L, a consultant at the Society for Biophysical Medicine, explains:

By stimulating the production of natural pain-relieving substances within the body, daily acupuncture acts as a substitute for heroin.

He feels that this treatment could be given on a large scale; the equipment – electro-acupuncture – is very simple and the treatment does not take long. However, detoxification by means of acupuncture, although it helps the addict to feel better almost at once without any toxic side-effects, is only the first step on the long road back to life without drugs. And isolated sessions, even every day, are often not enough to help him emerge from the whole lifestyle which accompanies his addiction.

Acupuncturist Mr S (Directory: London Road, Romford, Essex) warns:

> *I have found from experience of treating addicts in Rotterdam that to treat on a daily basis is not satisfactory. Treatment should be under controlled conditions necessitating needle applications three times a day over a minimum period of three to four weeks.*

He feels that, ideally, patients should be in hospital during withdrawal so that there is no chance for them to get more heroin.

This is backed up by Caroline K (Directory: Barbican Acupuncture Clinic, London EC2):

> *Acupuncture treatment does help with withdrawals, there's no doubt about it. But it's very difficult for them just to turn up for their treatment and stay off. There are all the social pressures, the emotional side; most addicts are in a couple, with one finding it easier to give up than the other. They would stand a much better chance of succeeding in a very well-run addiction unit, with staff to give them total continuous support, together with their treatments.*

Evonne F (Directory: Victoria Road, London NW6) feels that heroin addicts should move from the area and break with their past associates.

> *Even if you take them off and they are the picture of health, all they need to do is run into one of their cronies in the street. 'Come on. You're so well now, one won't do you any harm!' And they'll give in, they'll start back on the old road again.*

One of the most interesting and successful practitioners in the field of addiction is the Scottish surgeon Meg Patterson, who uses a technique she has developed from acupuncture which she calls Neuro-Electric Therapy. This grew out of her discovery, in 1972, that opiate addicts in a Hong Kong hospital suffered minimal withdrawal symptoms when they were treated with electro-acupuncture. Reasoning that acupuncture is an electrical phenomenon, and that the ancient theory of energy coursing round the body in channels called meridians refers to electrical fields, she replaced the needles with electrodes and experimented with various aspects of the electrical signal. She has found that different addictions respond to different electrical frequencies and that her musician patients – she has treated many rock stars – are able to home in on the right frequencies straight away.

She gives her addicts small, transistorized machines, with two leads attached to adhesive electrodes which are worn behind the ears and which carry a minute electrical current. The patient wears his 'black box' for several days, during which the right frequency for him persuades the brain to start up endorphin production again. (This technique has nothing to do with ECT, or electro-convulsive therapy.) In her book *Hooked?* Dr Patterson writes:

> *Now, for the first time, it is possible for addicts to be detoxified from any chemical form of addiction, in only ten days, with minimal discomfort. NET is also the first treatment ever to reverse the long-term chronic withdrawal syndrome, which may last for many months, in addition to dealing with the acute withdrawal syndrome.*

But NET, like all other detoxification techniques, is a valuable tool – not a complete cure. Dr Patterson realizes that, after the rapid detoxification of NET, the patient is confronted by the problems that led to his addiction in the first place, and writes:

> *A definition of cure for which I would prefer to be judged is the healing in body, mind and spirit, of those who were previously unable to function responsibly because of substance abuse.*

Healing

Ian G (Directory: Haley Street, London SW3) uses a combination of healing and counselling.

> *How I explain healing to people is in this way: you have a television set which transforms invisible picture waves into something that you can see, and you have a healer who transforms and directs that invisible healing energy, too. I believe that the power of healing, which I refer to as love, is able to affect body chemistry and mind together. Eventually, one can transmute whatever it is within the person's psyche that leads them to need chemical substances. There's a common thread I find going through all addicts – a terrific lack of self-esteem. The slightest thing and they will go off on a guilt trip, and ironing this out takes a long time, I find. But healing and*

counselling are a powerful combination – and I have been very lucky with the intrinsic quality of the people who have been coming to me.

Homoeopathy

Evonne F uses acupuncture, homoeopathy and counselling and has treated many heroin and cocaine addicts. Homoeopathy treats the whole individual and takes account of his personality as well as the illness.

You need all the nuances of the person to be able to pinpoint the actual homoeopathic remedy; there can be a whole range of remedies. Now, we have lots of food additives, and a child of only ten can already have a suppressive history of treatment because of antibiotics too. You need to uproot all that to start with. That by itself produces a massive change in personality, confidence and so on. With a cocaine or heroin addict, you need to deal with the psychological aspects together with the physical damage; you need to find the causative factor that started the addiction, whether it is lack of confidence and fear of meeting strangers, or whatever it is.

Hypnotherapy

Hypnotherapist Alastair B (Directory: Hypno-Analysis Centre of West London, 31, Harley Street, London W1), takes the same approach.

With hypno-analysis, one gets to the cause of addiction. The best example is the oil pressure light on your car. When it comes on, you could quite easily smash the light or unscrew the valve to make it go out; but you don't. Much better to adjust the oil pressure itself.

He is one of the few alternative practitioners who supports prescribed methadone for a short time, but agrees that it's another step again to get an addict off methadone. He has found that heroin addicts make unreliable patients and that helping them is difficult.

Basically, I would treat a heroin addict like an alcoholic; I would not try to take them off the heroin. I would hope that someone else was doing that. Where we can help is in the drying-out process. But we're not dealing in magic. Someone does have to come in regularly for treatment.

A 1986 report[7] describes hypnotherapy successfully given to a 20-year-old girl who was a heroin addict. But she was also shown how to meditate and given intense support. Her whole personality was treated, not just her addiction.

Transcendental Meditation

I spoke to TM teacher Roger L (Directory: Nationwide):

Meditation is more effective if you are not taking drugs. Normally we say to people that it would be a good idea to wait until they come off non-prescribed drugs before starting TM. But obviously if they are addicted that is an unreasonable request. So we will teach TM to someone who is addicted, but only with social, family and environmental support as part of the programme. Heroin addicts need a lot of follow-up; they have all sorts of problems which they feel impinge. However, we did teach a group of about 25 people at a drug centre and the results were very good. Some of them are still meditating now.

Several research projects confirm that meditation, with its effects on mind, body and spirit, tends to reduce drug-taking in general, including the use of illegal hard drugs.[8] Those who take drugs often cease their habit without any effort after an average of two years' practice of TM.

Massage

Acupuncturist Caroline K also trained in massage and recommends it for addicts.

It would be very useful in drug treatment centres to give everyone a massage every day; it affects the whole nervous system, the brain, and relaxes the person in quite a profound way.

Nutrition

Dr Alexander Schauss, director of the American Institute for Biosocial Research, is a pioneer researcher into the way food affects our behaviour. He writes that addicts usually have 'atrocious diets and are addicted to sweets . . . In over ten years, I have not worked with one addict, whether juvenile or adult, who has consumed even a marginally nutritious diet.'[9]

Low blood sugar usually accompanies addiction. The blood sugar is forced up too quickly by eating foods full of refined sugar and then plummets down again afterwards, causing fatigue and more cravings for sweet foods. To avoid this, take small meals, with snacks in between if you wish. Choose from the following foods: protein (cheese, milk, yoghurt, eggs, nuts, fish, meat); fresh fruit, salads and vegetables; and whole grains (wholemeal bread, brown rice and other unrefined cereals, wholegrain crispbread). If you take fruit juice, always accompany it with some food. Avoid *all* added sugars, including brown sugar and honey. Cut down all junk and convenience foods, sweets and chocolate, coffee and tea as much as you can. Try a little powdered brewer's yeast (preferably containing chromium) in some juice.

The substance most needed by the body to get rid of the toxic effects of drugs is vitamin C, and not surprisingly many doctors find it valuable for addiction. Doctors Libby and Stone gave heroin addicts huge does of C (between 25 and 85 grams a day), together with other supplements, and reported that all their patients lost their craving.[10] This was confirmed in other research using vitamin C and minerals, carried out by the San Francisco Drug Treatment Program to help withdrawing methadone addicts.[11] Dr Jordan Scher has also used large doses of vitamin C for methadone addiction.

Vic Pawlek, working at a drug treatment centre in Phoenix, Arizona, successfully used 3 grams of vitamins C and B_3 every day for addictions.[9] Dr William H. Philpott, director of the Philpott Medical Center in Oklahoma City, gives intravenous doses of vitamin C, with several B vitamins and minerals, and states that 'even heroin addicts can tolerate withdrawal with the help of these.'[13]

A case history: Carol

'My boyfriend John and I were heroin addicts for four years, and we'd often tried to come off. We even went down to Somerset for a bit once to get away from the drug scene. We had been on methadone, too.

'During all that time I was a musician and I was in John's band, so we had plenty of money. We had a record deal too, so our drug use never caused us to steal, become prostitutes, all the things that make people fall apart.

'To this day, I don't know why we became addicts. There was so much of it, we just fell into it. And when you become an addict, in the end all your friends are addicts too. You just close ranks, you don't see anybody else.

'Anyway, in the end we went to our doctor, who is a homoeopath. We told him we were addicts and we didn't want any more drugs. He told us to choose a day to stop using and book appointments with various alternative practitioners from that day. I had never had this kind of treatment before; I was terrified of going to an acupuncturist – I thought the needles were about 6 inches long. I said to my doctor, 'What is reflexology?' I said 'no-one's going to touch my feet because I'm ticklish.' As for the healer, I wasn't going anywhere where I could have religion laid on me.

'He gave us injections of arnica each for shock. When you come off, you are in shock. He gave us vitamins, too, and he said, "Do you trust me?" I said I did. He said, "You've tried everything else; methadone, running away to the country. This may be of some use to you. What's the alternative? I don't know what else to do for you."

'I liked that. He hadn't said, "This is going to work." He'd been honest with us.

'So there we were, both doing it together, trying to come off yet again. We went to an acupuncturist, a reflexologist, a hypnotherapist, a healer. All in a couple of weeks. I was not just going blindly, full of faith, to these people; I had a huge degree of scepticism. We both did.

'For the first few days we didn't sleep at all. It was horrible. Withdrawal is not very nice, but it's not the end of the world. Part of the problem with heroin addiction is the romance that is built up around withdrawal – cold turkey – and about how ghastly it is, which of course it isn't; it's not life-threatening. But all this time, when we were having treatments, we felt very positive, very different from all the other times when we'd stopped. One of the symptoms is that you shiver, you are freezing, but you pour with sweat as well. All the therapists had asked us how many times a day we were bathing, but I couldn't go near the bath. I thought that if we'd had someone then to bathe us, rub our shoulders, it would have helped, but we were too ill to do anything ourselves. It was very painful.

'We just stuck it. In a few days we started to feel more optimistic. So we thought, if it works for us, perhaps it will work for somebody else. We started saying to some of our friends, "Look, we did it. Why don't you try it this way?"

'We found that some therapies we needed more than others. Reflexology for instance; it's important to have at least six sessions. Coming off suppresses all the body's functions and none of them can work properly. I still have acupuncture once a month.

'Looking back, taking heroin is an anti-life thing to do. It shuts down your understanding, narrows it. Heroin addiction is a full-time job, a 24-hour search to get it which overrides everything. When you become a heroin addict, they could blow up London for all you care.

'There's no doubt in my mind that the alternative treatments we had were a turning point. The withdrawals weren't so bad, we felt more positive all the time, and we stayed off. We have been off for two years now.

'We have opened this centre now for addicts (Directory: Lisson Cottages, London NW1). We put people on to alternative practitioners for treatment and we give them a lot of help ourselves. That's the good thing that's come out of it.'

Some advice on coming off

Your first step is to plan how you are going to come off heroin.

You will know that, although coming off is an extremely unpleasant process, it will not kill you, and that withdrawals, both from heroin and from methadone, can be minimized in various drugless ways. Take time deciding which method you are going to use, and don't be afraid to ask questions before you choose your treatment.

Recognize that, as a withdrawing addict, you are very vulnerable. You must also remember that replacing one drug with another – tobacco, or alcohol – may be a temporary prop, but it's a short-sighted thing to do; any mood-altering substance will make it more likely for you to weaken and go back on heroin again.

You will probably find that any emotional problems you had when you started using will surface again now. They must eventually be dealt with but, again, you are very vulnerable now, so take it gently, be kind to yourself. Try to be aware of the guilt that so often plagues addicts, and detach yourself from it. You can be sure that everyone you see in the street has done something he or she is ashamed of and regrets, so you are not unique. You are not alone, either; a support group may well be essential for you now, and if so you will find the Directory useful. It's best to assume that heroin will have sapped your powers to make decisions and stick to them to some extent, so don't be ashamed to ask for all the help you need.

The second, and final step is staying off. A purely physical addiction to heroin can be overcome in a matter of months and the body will return to normal. But a psychological addiction takes longer. If long-term heroin use was part of your life, giving it up, and staying without it, will be a revolutionary change and, however much help you get, you are the only one who can make that change. Ian G has this to say about coming off heroin:

Taken the right way, it can be the turning point. You sometimes have to get to the lowest ebb of addiction before coming up, and coming up is to embrace yourself spiritually and go on. There's a tremendous potential amongst these people for great good. There is a great contribution for them to make.

So coming off is a real, solid opportunity for you to change your life for the better. The first step – giving up – is vital, but in a sense it's only the honeymoon. Staying off – an even greater accomplishment – is the marriage. Being an ex-addict is a terrific achievement.

Heroin and the family

Addiction has an effect on the whole family. Nowadays it's part of parents' responsibility to find out about drugs before they need to so that they understand the problems.

Schools are offering more information now on drug abuse, and your local health authority, your GP and your local library may be able to help.

Signs of heroin use are: mood changes, sleepiness, pinpoint pupils of eyes; loss of appetite and interest in hobbies and school friends; lying or stealing, nausea, vomiting, headaches, dizziness, lots of colds, coughs and chills, slurred speech and insomnia; any unusual smells, stains or marks on the body, with unfamiliar powder, capsules, tinfoil, needles or syringes found lying about.

The trouble with many of these signs is that they could apply simply to the ordinary ups and downs of growing up, so you will have to use your judgement and the knowledge you already have of your child. The fact that you are a parent and this is not just a stranger but your own flesh and blood is going to mean that you are very emotionally involved, and you may be inclined to fear the worst when there is really nothing to worry about, or you may find proof of drug use and over-react to that. Being detached about this problem is the hardest thing to do, but is very necessary.

Blowing your top, blaming the child, lecturing or trying to cover up for him will drive him into a corner where he will feel defensive, isolated, and dramatic. These are just the feelings that encourage more use of the drug.

You may feel that it's all your fault. But adolescence is a time of experimentation and this is part of that urge. It is also probably a way round the pain of growing up that we all have to go through.

The young person involved is the only one who can decide he wants to stop taking heroin. Be calm, supportive, and give him confidence in his ability to make the right decision and to go about it, with your help, in the right way. He already knows in his heart that it is infinitely better to face life without the double-edged sword of an addictive and destructive chemical.

Please see the directory for more information.

References

1 *Young People and Heroin: An examination of heroin use in the North of England*, Research report No. 8, Geoffrey Pearson, Mark Gilman and Shirley McIver.
2 *Hooked? NET: The new approach to drug cure*, Meg Patterson, MBE MBCh.B, FRCSE (Faber and Faber, 1986).
3 *Medicines: A guide for everybody*, Peter Parish (Penguin Books, 1984).
4 J. M. Brown and J. W. Strachen, *British Medical Journal*, 288 (1983).
5 Dr V. Clement Jones et al, *Lancet*, 2 (1979).
6 M. M. P. Yang et al, *American Journal of Chinese Medicine*, 2.
7 Thomas H. P. Vandamme, *Australian Journal of Clinical and Experimental Hypnosis*, 14 (1986).
8 A. and E. N. Aron, *Addictive Behaviours*, 5 (1980).
  A. and E. N. Aron, *Bulletin of the Society of Psychologists in*

Addictive Behaviours, 2:1; 28-33 (1983).

M. Shafii et al, *American Journal of Psychiatry*, 132 (1975).

9 *Diet, Crime and Delinquency*, Alexander Schauss (Parker House, 1980).

10 A. Libby and I. Stone, *Journal of Orthomolecular Psychiatry*, 6:4 (1977).

11 V. Free et al, *Journal of Orthomolecular Psychiatry*, 7:4 (1978).

12 J. Scher et al, *Journal of Orthomolecular Psychiatry*, 5:3 (1976).

13 Interviewed in the American magazine *Bestways* (May 1982).

Nicotine

Inhaling smoke for kicks goes back several thousand years to the ancient Egyptians and to the Mayan Indians of South America, who used burning herbs to produce trances and ecstatic states.

By Elizabethan times, tobacco smoking had spread to Europe. When Sir Walter Raleigh was first discovered smoking at home, a servant threw a bucket of water over him.

Now, about 100,000 people in the UK die every year from tobacco-related diseases[1] and, thanks to its bad press, smoking is on the way out. But although smokers are now in the minority – only 34 per cent of all adults smoke – the 11- to 16-year olds are doing the tobacco companies a good turn by spending between £70 and £90 million a year on cigarettes. Among 14- to 15-year old girls, smoking is even increasing.[2]

What smoking does

Smoking makes us feel good, otherwise nobody would do it. As well as temporarily stimulating the brain, it causes the release of endorphins, the natural hormones which relieve pain and depression. So we feel alert, relaxed, and able to cope. Although the first few puffs rouse us, relieving boredom and fatigue, more smoking sedates.

A cigarette is a supportive piece of equipment. It gives us confidence at parties when we feel awkward, and perhaps this is one of the reasons smoking is so popular with the young. In the boom days of smoking, the old advertisement 'You're never alone with a Strand' dramatized the cigarette. It was part of being aloof, knowing, of being street smart. In the older films the ritual of opening a cigarette case – preferably an expensive one – and getting out a cigarette and lighting it was frequently part of the action and heightened the suspense. The girl accepts a light, the man touches her hand and she gives him a smouldering look ... Perhaps the death of this mythology is another reason for the current departure of the cigarette.

Now let's look at what a cigarette does to us (or a cigar or a pipe. Four cigars, or four pipefuls are the toxic equivalent of 10 cigarettes[3]). Remember that *all* cigarettes are harmful, even the low-tar ones.

A smoker takes in several thousand different chemical compounds, including carbon monoxide, nitrogen dioxide and hydrogen cyanide. Some are irritants or carcinogens. The irritants foul the lungs and can cause phlegm and bronchitis, and the tars which stain fingers are carcinogenic. Carbon monoxide, the main gas in cigarette smoke, can exceed the permitted industrial level by eight times. It reduces the blood's ability to transport oxygen and strains the heart.

The only addictive substance in tobacco is nicotine.

Nicotine has contradictory effects. As well as releasing endorphins it immediately stimulates the output of adrenalin and noradrenalin. These stress hormones put up the blood pressure and heart rate, constrict blood vessels and increase blood sugar and fats, preparing the body for emergency action. Then the nicotine calms the brain, stopping adrenalin flow and impeding nerve transmission along muscles. So, after a high, we get a let-down feeling and reach for another cigarette.

Smoking stops stomach contractions, reducing hunger, and puts up the metabolic rate so that a smoker uses up about 10 per cent more calories.[4] People who stop often put on weight for the time being.

Nicotine cuts down blood oxygen. This robs the tissues and can cause an arterial disease, intermittent claudication. Smoking paralyses the little hairs, or cilia, lining the windpipe and bronchial tubes, which sweep mucus and debris upwards and out of the body. When you stop smoking, the cilia start working again. Nicotine also increases the stickiness of blood platelets and destroys lecithin, a soapy substance which breaks down fats and helps to control blood cholesterol levels. *Smokers are twice as likely to die from heart disease as non-smokers.*

Smoking can damage the unborn child and may cause genetic damage. Nicotine gets into breast milk, and women who smoke are less likely to conceive[5] and probably more likely to develop cervical cancer.

Smoking can cause calcium loss and increased acidity in the bones so that structural minerals drain away, with the risk of bone disease. It impairs eyesight, manual dexterity, reflexes, exercise tolerance and immunity. Heavy smoking can cause reduced vision (tobacco amblyopia) due to the inactivation of vitamin B_{12}.[6] Smoking also makes you more prone to gum disease.[7]

These well-publicized risks mean that, over the past ten years, one in five smokers has stopped.

Other ways of getting nicotine

Some people think that, if they're not actually smoking, they're all right. But chewing tobacco can cause appalling damage to the gums and can eventually lead to mouth cancer. Also, contrary to what some American athletes believe, snuff raises blood pressure and slows reaction time.[8]

Clearly, it is better to give up addictive nicotine altogether rather than simply finding other ways of taking it.[10]

Stopping

Twelve to twenty-four hours after a smoker has stopped, carbon monoxide and nicotine have been largely eliminated by the body and the circulatory system and heart are in better shape. Six weeks without tobacco allow T-cell immune activity to return to normal.[9] Two months later, there is an improvement in small airway diseases such as asthma. But although tobacco does not affect physical functioning as drastically as heroin or tranquillizers, or change personality and the way we perceive reality, it may take over ten years to remove a long-established nicotine addiction from every cell in the body.

Nicotine withdrawal can cause restlessness and insomnia, headaches, constipation, impaired memory and judgement, and decreased heart rate. These symptoms – which do not happen to everyone – may persist for between forty-eight hours and three weeks.

Orthodox treatment

A chewing gum, Nicorette, is available from doctors on a private prescription. It contains nicotine in a buffered resin, and it does help some people to stop smoking. The few side-effects – mouth irritation, nausea and indigestion, and flatulence – usually wear off quickly. However, various clinical trials give differing results on its efficacy, and between five and ten per cent of Nicorette users still need to chew it after one year.[10]

Drugless treatments

Acupuncture

Acupuncture is the commonest approach. Acupuncturist Caroline K (Directory: Barbican, London EC2) says:

Acupuncture definitely eases withdrawals. A lot of patients have tightness in the chest when they stop. That's partly emotional. Their tension affects their breathing, which becomes shallow. The treatment takes away a lot of chest discomfort and helps control smoker's cough. It helps prevent headaches and irritability from building up because it's very relaxing. After a lot of smoking, nicotine conditions the body in so many different ways that when you take it away there are quite uncomfortable withdrawal symptoms.

But in my experience it doesn't stop the classic feeling of depression that a lot of smokers get. When I was being trained I was told that this must come out and that the acupuncture mustn't suppress it. I think that the smoking is very much a matter of kept-in sadness and tension; you breathe it in, you stuff it down into your body, into your lungs, and when you finally stop smoking it all comes back out again. In Chinese medicine, the lungs relate to grief and sadness. Crying is fairly common when smokers give up.

I treat a lot of smokers now. I use the standard points for nicotine, and an ordinary diagnosis as well, working on any other problem they might have and giving a whole-body treatment, thinking very much about relaxing them. The more relaxed you are, the less you will want to pick up a cigarette. I also use a small stud which I put in one ear. They press the stud at least three times a day, and whenever else they need it. Some people need to touch it a lot and some more or less forget about it. The studs are just tiny needles, like drawing pins, and I put a cosmetic plaster on top so they don't show.

With me, they get at least four treatments. They need a lot of support because they have been leaning heavily on smoking. If they feel you are there, that's half the battle won.

I spoke to Dr Richard R who took the unusual step of studying traditional acupuncture while he was at medical school (Directory: Isis Alternative Health Resources, London N17).

I think it's useful to think in terms of four aspects of addiction to tobacco; maybe this applies to other addictions too. First is the chemical addiction to the nicotine, second is the sheer force of habit and the patterns of behaviour; third is social forces – people constraining you to smoke, and the fourth is more complicated, and falls under the general heading of psychology. People smoke to push their emotions under the carpet. These factors are all quite different and need different interventions to help.

I think acupuncture is quite good for the first factor, the nicotine withdrawal, which lasts a few days. Acupuncture designed to help the person balance his energies will help. There are special formula addiction points, and there are press needles for the ear, usually in the lung point or the relaxation point in the ear lobes. I work intuitively with these aspects.

The day they come to see me, I will encourage them not to stop smoking that day. At this consultation we discuss exactly what their smoking habit is about. I get them to keep a record of when they smoke for a few days and, when I see them again, we can both see what the habit patterns are, and design ways to deal with them. If, for example, they always smoke when they pick up the 'phone, I say, 'OK, make sure there are no cigarettes within reach, or stick a little notice on your cigarette packet saying 'Stop', or 'Do you really need this – or is it habit?' and so on. They can inform themselves more and more this way. Likewise with social constraints; it's a matter of strategy, tactics, and of occasionally remembering.

The relaxation comes in later, with the fourth category, the psychological. When a person is just giving up smoking it is not a good time for them to try to relax; they are very tense. Usually there's suppressed anger, irritability, coming out.

I also recommend three grams of vitamin C a day to help the body clear the toxins out, and a large daily dose of B complex. I ask them to give up caffeine, too, in tea and coffee, and ask that they avoid meat. It helps if you can get the person to jolt himself out of his usual habit patterns, such as a meat diet, smoking, and coffee. This makes it easier for him to give up.

Garnett S (Directory: Woodhouse Road, London N12) also links smoking with coffee.

> *You nearly always find that smokers are coffee drinkers; if you're going to stop them smoking, you've got to get them to cut down on the coffee at the same time. To begin with, there's an interview. I ask how many do they smoke. I ask what stress they are under at the moment and how life is in general. You have to give up at the right time for you. I have to make you confident, make you feel that I can help you. But it's your willpower that's going to do it. All I'm going to do is help your withdrawals, cut them to a minimum.*
>
> *It can feel rotten for the first couple of weeks. You can have a horrible taste in your mouth, a headache, your stomach doesn't feel too good; the nervous system has got to go through a change – no longer is it going to have all that lovely nicotine. When you get down to a certain level you can override it; the desire to smoke becomes less and less.*
>
> *I would treat you with electro-acupuncture. You would come in for the first two weeks, three times a week. I don't stick to rules, I look at the person. On average after that you could probably have a couple of sessions a week for two weeks, then once a week. By six weeks you should be OK.*

A three-month trial in Singapore found that ear acupuncture using a laser was effective against smoking.[9] In a similar Russian trial, also using laser acupuncture, 71 per cent of the volunteers stopped smoking completely.[11] Research reported in *The Practitioner* gave less spectacular, but still good, results: 18 per cent stopped.[12]

Hypnotherapy

Antonia C (Directory: Rochester Square, London NW1) comments that 'hypnotherapy is mainly for smoking addiction. It's particularly effective using the latest methods.' She does not advocate the 'grit your teeth' approach.

> *People have failed by using only willpower; when you fight something it becomes more attractive to you. For instance, if you say to someone 'Don't whatever you do think of pink elephants,' they will immediately think of pink elephants. They can't help it. The same thing happens if they are constantly thinking, 'I mustn't smoke, it's bad for me. I mustn't smoke.' It becomes an obsession, and so more and more compelling.*

The first thing we do is find out what purpose the smoking is serving. Every impulse is serving some purpose. For some people, it is filling a need in their lives – almost like a friend. It is always there when everything else lets them down. With some people – especially women – it can be a defiant thing; the only thing they can do if they've got overbearing husbands. It's their little game; their husband has no control over this one thing. So in the first session I find out what purpose it is serving.

Then I introduce them to the creative part of the mind, the part that's operating when they do anything successful, the part that gives them the right intuitions. I get that subsconscious part to come in and create new, alternative, behaviours in place of smoking.

So, you get into their world, get into the way they are thinking and feeling. and you put them in touch with the positive, capable, powerful parts of themselves, and bring those parts in to create new behaviours. Some therapists used to tell the client that he would feel sick and horrible when he had a smoke. This is aversion therapy, but it can cause a lot of anxiety. So instead you introduce positive feelings; you get them to remember times when they felt particularly confident and happy, a real peak experience in their lives, and then you go on to say 'every time now that you take a cigarette out of the packet and put it back unlit, you will have the same wonderful feeling.' You can build this up – feelings of pride, self-esteem, happiness – any experience they have had which is very positive. Rather than fighting the habit, therefore, you are changing their thinking to make them realize how wonderful it is to be in control, to be taking care of themselves. I also talk a little about what tobacco does to the body.

This approach has been proved to be the most effective one, but an addiction to smoking is a tough one. So besides that I use visualization techniques, imagining the body being cleansed. You are using their mind, not imposing; that's very important, the basis of all modern hypnotherapy. More and more we are finding that, if you let them create the changes, make the visualization themselves, it's very effective. People who give up will sometimes say to me, 'That's the part that really got me.' By the third session, they begin to feel happy that they are not going to smoke again.

Some people believe they cannot be hypnotized, but John B (Directory: Willingdon, East Sussex) disagrees.

Virtually everyone can be hypnotized. It's as easy as breathing. It relieves the tension to some extent and is particularly useful where the tobacco is a masking drug for a neurosis. I had one woman who had to smoke because, when she was at school, she hung her coat on the wrong peg once, and this sparked off her neurosis.

Who is untreatable? Someone sent by his wife, just coming to keep her happy. Or a person who is trying to prove that their addiction is stronger than anything, even hypnosis. The patient must have a positive attitude, must want to give up. But it's quite wrong to suggest that it is easy to stop smoking without help.

London hypnotherapist Gloria M (Directory: Chiltern Street, London W1) adds:

Hypnosis, like relaxation and meditation to some extent, is a physical technique. The brain starts to work in a slightly different way, oxygen consumption and pulse rate go down. The hypnotist can teach a person how to relax and they can make use of this technique for themselves.

I don't really believe in addiction. People who smoke are doing it for some reason; it's doing something for them. Some find that it helps concentration, for example. The clue to helping people is to help them find something else more positive in terms of health or saving money, something they will get out of not smoking. These are the ones who succeed. They see it in terms of getting something better. Believing or not believing that they can stop is quite irrelevant, but the person really has to want to stop.

American research[13] found hypnosis to be effective to varying degrees in helping volunteers to give up smoking.

Herbal medicine

Medical herbalist Julian B (Directory: The Wilbury Clinic of Natural Medicine, Hove, Sussex) used to be a chain smoker and thinks it is useful to be an ex-addict. He tries to define addiction:

I think it's a once-removed phenomenon; what you really want is something else which you can't define, so this sets up a hunger for tobacco instead. I think that spiritual hunger may be a part of it, and then there's the hunger for oral satisfaction.

Like most other practitioners, he does not depend on the patient's willpower

The greatest ally is humour. Humour is changed perspective, and if

you can get the patient to see what they are doing in the form of a joke, you are in a different world; you have a different way of approaching it. The other thing is to always ask him to make only promises that he can keep. The first one is: 'I will ask myself before I smoke, "Do I really want this cigarette?"' I suggest then that, if they smoke at all, it's through ginger, or peppermint, or whatever else is going to make it taste foul. And I tell them to take out a cigarette, pretend to light it, then put it to their lips and pretend to take a puff. I think smokers have got a lot of tension in the diaphragm and this relieves that.

H. H. Zeylstra, Director of the School of Herbal Medicine in Tunbridge Wells, tells me that several herbs can be used for addiction as a tonic for the nervous system and that extract of lobelia contains alkaloids which produce unpleasant results if you smoke a cigarette.

Transcendental meditation

TM teacher Roger L (Directory: Nationwide) commented briefly on the difference between addiction and choice.

Almost all the meditators I know who smoke – and it's only a handful – smoke because they want to. I think that's a big difference. Even then, they generally stop eventually. We say to people who come along that if they want to stop it will be easier with TM.

Research published in 1976 reported a decrease in cigarette smoking following TM.[14]

Neutralization

This 'hair of the dog' approach consists of giving the patient a minute dose of the substance to which he is addicted, which acts to turn off his craving. Dr David L, consulting allergist (Directory: The Northwest Allergy Clinic, Bolton, Lancashire) uses neutralization together with a strict diet.

One patient, a heavy smoker, had an immediate response to nicotine neutralization. Within minutes of receiving the neutralization dilution she lost all urge for a cigarette, and the effect lasted, as predicted, as long as the neutralization lasted (about 24 hours in her case). The dose is given daily until desensitization occurs. I must admit that spectacular responses like that are rare, but most patients find that alkaloid and food neutralization alleviate the addictions to some extent. Very few patients find it impossible to give up the foods we tell them to give up, however strong the cravings. But we do have our total failures as well.

Alister B (Directory: 31, Harley Street, London W1) used the same approach.

The patient brings in small quantities of everything, then we use an extremely diluted version of the substance to turn the person's reaction off. For tobacco, we have a success rate of 86 per cent; American statistics claim that this rate drops to about 52 per cent after one year.

His treatment also includes hypnotherapy to relax his patient.

I say, 'Let's forget about the smoking to begin with. We need to get rid of your anxiety and tension first, then we will think about taking away the smoking.'

Dr Harold T (Directory: Rutt House Clinic, Ivybridge, Devon), who also uses neutralization, emphasizes that 'addiction and allergy march hand in hand.' A person can develop a 'masked allergy' to a food or a drug, which means that he has outgrown his first, unpleasant reaction to it and is now addicted. If he goes without it, he will suffer withdrawal symptoms. This can be seen when a teenager tries his first cigarette. He coughs and feels queasy, but after repeated attempts he starts to enjoy it, and after a while he finds that he needs it. Many practitioners feel that any substance to which a person is addicted is also a masked allergen to him.

The pioneer of this approach, allergy expert Dr Richard Mackarness, is now running a clinic in Australia and uses neutralization to treat nicotine addiction. From 200 answers to enquiries which he sent out to ex-patients, about 25 per cent have stopped smoking altogether, 50 per cent have cut down to safer levels, and 25 per cent have gone back to heavy smoking again.[15] (For further information on this technique, please see *A Little of What You Fancy* by Richard Mackarness, (Fontana Books, 1985).)

Osteopathy and cranial osteopathy

Osteopath Susan T (Directory: Meopham, Kent) says:

With a smoker I'd use osteopathy with probably cranial osteopathy as well. There is always a high level of stress in their systems and the base of the skull is usually very tight; the diaphragm isn't working very well, either.

But I also use affirmations and visualization, which are something they can do for themselves. For instance, they say to themselves, 'I trust myself to be healthy and happy; I enjoy not smoking now.' Then they take three or four good, deep breaths when they really want a cigarette. After going through all that first, it's amazing how often a cigarette seems too much bother!

Nicotine and food

When we smoke, nicotine taken into the lungs is rapidly distributed throughout the body in the bloodstream and some is eventually eliminated in the urine. The normal pH of urine varies from between -4.5 in the acid range (counting up to a neutral 0) and $+8$ in the alkaline range, and this balance is constantly being adjusted. When the urine is on the acid side, it can excrete almost all the nicotine available to it. This can be as much as half the amount taken in. (Incidentally, stress makes the urine more acid.) But the more alkaline the urine is, the more nicotine can be re-absorbed by the body and circulated round again.

Scientists have now confirmed that, with higher levels of alkalinity, smokers are less likely to crave more nicotine. To establish this, Stanley Schachter, Professor of Psychology at Columbia University in New York, and James Fix of the University of Nebraska College of Medicine gave large doses of an alkalinizing agent, bicarbonate of soda, to groups of smokers. They were subsequently able to cut down on cigarettes.[16]

However, because of possible kidney damage, it is not wise to go on taking enormous doses of bicarbonate of soda and, commenting on this research, nutritional biochemist Jack Smith said, 'the real benefit is when you *change people's diets to produce an alkaline balance*' [my italics]. He also pointed out that a diet high in alkaline foods – vegetables, fruit and salads – would be relatively low in calories, and that this would minimize the weight gain which many people notice when they stop smoking. (This whole theory is discussed in *The Stop Smoking Diet* by Jane Ogle, Piatkus Books, 1982.)

Here are contrasting lists of foods which encourage alkalinity and acidity in the body. These lists are necessarily incomplete, and I have left out many foods in the middle range, but you can see the kinds of foods which will help. Figures vary widely, so only extremes have been quoted.

The most alkaline-forming food on this list is molasses, at about +60.0 on the scale, and the least is bananas, at about +8.0.

Alkaline-forming foods

Molasses	Avocados
Raisins	Pineapple
Spinach	Broccoli
Cantaloupe melon	Fresh apricots
Haricot beans	Soybean flour
Brewer's yeast	Cucumbers
Dried figs	Grapes
Beetroot	Nectarines
Brussels sprouts	Lettuce
Blackberries	Turnip
Almonds	Cherries
Dried apricots	Grapefuit
Potatoes	Oranges
Carrots	Bananas

You may be surprised to see citrus fruits listed. The acid in these and other fruits is excreted by the body soon after they have been eaten and the residue is alkaline.

Acid-forming foods

Crabmeat	Pork
Alcohol	Veal
Lobster	Calf's liver
Scallops	Trout
Mussels	Chicken
Wheat germ	Haddock
Oysters	Beef
Lentils	Eggs

The most acid-forming food on the above list is crabmeat, at about −34.0, and the least is eggs, at about −9.0.

Although wheatgerm is very acid, and soybean flour is on the alkaline-forming list, other cereals are further down the acid scale below eggs, as are cheeses. Butter, tea, coffee and sugar are neutral and milk is slightly alkaline.

Sprouting seeds and grains

This part of the nutritional approach is very important. Get some seeds and grains from a health food store (not a seed merchant, where they will have been chemically treated) and put a handful in an old jam jar with a muslin top, or use a plastic sprouter. Soak them in water overnight and then rinse them twice a day; in a few days the sprouts will be ready to eat. A useful guide is *The Complete Sprouting Book* by Per and Gita Sellman (Thorsons, 1984).

Sprouting seeds and grains are among the most alkaline-forming, and nourishing foods known. During sprouting, vitamin C, a major detoxifier, increases by 60 per cent in cereals and several hundred per cent in some bean sprouts. There is 200 per cent more B_2 in wheat sprouts than in wheat grain, 90 per cent more B_3, and 30 per cent more B_5. Alfalfa is particularly rich in calcium. Protective factors called pacifarins have been identified in these foods and they are high in protein. They are packed with all the nutrients you need to throw off the poisons in tobacco.

Sprouting seeds and grains can be added to breakfast cereals, scrambled eggs, soups, casseroles and salads, or they can be eaten by themselves. They are best eaten raw. Have them growing in the kitchen and try to add a good handful to every meal.

American doctor John Douglass finds that a tobacco addiction can lose its grip after a few weeks on a predominantly alkaline-forming raw diet. So make sure that raw fruits and vegetables comprise at least half, and preferably three-quarters, of your diet (cooking reduces nutritional content). Try this way of eating for at least four weeks and, when you have cut down on your smoking or, better still, stopped, follow a modified form. Over-acidity is involved in many diseases and this raw, fresh diet is the best possible for your general health.

Some researchers believe that low blood sugar accompanies

addiction, so small, frequent meals are better than large, infrequent ones.

Please try not to replace your need to smoke with a need for coffee. Coffee causes a rapid lift and subsequent let-down similar to that caused by nicotine.

Sunflower seeds

One of the problems with smoking is that you get used to having something in your mouth. A good way round this is to chew a handful of sunflower seeds.

Sunflower seeds mimic some of the effects of nicotine, but they are nourishing and not addictive. Smoking gives a lift partly because it causes an increase in blood sugar and stimulates adrenal output. Sunflower seeds give energy too and are mildly stimulating, but without the subsequent drop into fatigue, so they make an excellent snack, and help to avoid low blood sugar.

Irritability is one of nicotine's withdrawal symptoms and sunflower seeds have most of the B vitamins to feed your nerves, as well as soothing oils. They are high in fibre too, and will alleviate constipation, which can be a withdrawal symptom. They also contain cystine from which a powerful detoxifier, L-cysteine, can be made by the body.

Dr Douglass recommends sunflower seeds to patients who are trying to give up smoking. Buy several bags of raw, unsalted seeds from a health food store (not a seed merchant) and help yourself when you crave a cigarette.

Supplements against smoking

Vitamin C has a major protective and detoxifying role in the body and is vital in an anti-smoking programme. Body levels of vitamin C are depressed in smokers; one cigarette destroys about 25 mg, almost the UK Recommended Daily Allowance (30 mg). The urine of heavy smokers is high in cinnabaric acid and vitamin C destoys both this carcinogen[17] and another in tobacco, benzopyrene.[18]

Take at least one gram of vitamin C a day, in two doses of 500 mg or more each, one after breakfast and one after lunch or tea. Some people find that vitamin C in its usual form, ascorbic acid, upsets the stomach. In this case take calcium ascorbate in the same dosage, obtainable from a health food store.

The whole range of B vitamins is essential, both to nourish your nerves and to enable the body to get rid of tobacco poisons. Brewer's yeast (the powder) is one of the best sources, but it tastes pretty peculiar, so go easy to start with. Try one teaspoonful a day in fruit juice or mixed in with your breakfast cereal, and work up to one dessertspoonful. Alternatively, take B-complex capsules at the maximum recommended dosage.

Amino acids, the building blocks of protein, are attracting much current interest and researchers are beginning to unravel their immense potential for treating illness. Histidine has been used for tobacco cravings; it also helps to relieve anxiety and tension, as does tryptophan. Both work on brain function to calm you down. Cystine protects against the damage done by smoking and helps the body to get rid of toxins in the nicotine. Tyrosine and phenylalanine help to replenish stress hormones, the lowered level of which, depleted by nicotine, cause depression when you stop smoking. Phenylalanine also helps to control the larger appetite which often accompanies stopping. Nicotine brings about an over-release of insulin, which in its turn forces the blood sugar down too low, so that you feel tired and long for another cigarette. Glutamine, glycine and lysine raise blood sugar levels to normal again.

Please note that amino acids as supplements should be taken only under the guidance of a practitioner who understands them.

A case history: Henry

'My job is quite pressured at times, but I started smoking long ago, when I was 14 or 15. I thought it was very daring of me. I'm 55 now, and I had stopped lots of times. Stopping is easy. The problem is, you start again. I'd be puffing away again almost the next day.

'Then a colleague of mine, a heavy smoker, died of lung cancer. I thought 'This is crazy,' and I asked my osteopath for some advice. He recommended Gloria M, a hypnotherapist. I didn't know what to expect. But I decided to give it a try.

'I went to her for about a month – six sessions in all. She would sit me down comfortably, make me close my eyes, and talk to me. She told me how to relax and so on; I still practise the relaxation myself, when things get a bit stressful.

'I stopped smoking after the first session, but I didn't really think I would keep it up, so I had more sessions. I stopped a year ago. I would love to be able to have the odd cigar from time to time, without going back on smoking all the time, but I don't trust myself yet.

'I think the treatment is a good thing and I am sure it has helped.'

Some advice on giving up

As the practitioners quoted above have said, there are many reasons why we want to smoke. It's not only an addiction to nicotine; there are other ways of needing a cigarette.

So, giving up may be easy – not everyone suffers from withdrawal symptoms – or it may be difficult and even frightening. We are all different. But please bear in mind that the more times you have tried to give it up, the more likely you are to succeed.

Having made the vital decision, please take it seriously, deciding what methods will suit you best, and see that you get as much help as you need from family, friends and practitioner.

Nobody can decide for you that this is the time to stop. You are responsible for this yourself. And remember – there are ten million people in the UK who used to smoke. You can become one of them.

Please see the directory for more information.

References

1 Action on Smoking and Health.
2 DHSS press release 85/338, dated 3 December 1985.
3 *Journal of the American Medical Association*, reported in *The Times*, 24 January 1986.
4 *New England Journal of Medicine* 314:2, reported in *The Times*, 14 January, 1986.
5 *British Medical Journal*, 290:6483.
6 *The Dictionary of Vitamins*, Dr Leonard Mervyn (Thorsons, 1984).
7 Research at Michigan University, reported in *The Times*, 22 July, 1983.

8 *Time* magazine, 15 July 1985.
9 *Journal of Alternative Medicine*, October 1986.
10 *Drug and Therapeutics Bulletin*, 27 August 1985.
11 *Journal of Alternative Medicine*, August, 1984
12 *The Practitioner*. March 1984.
13 A. F. Barabaz et al, *International Journal of Clinical and Experimental Hypnosis*, 34:3 (1986).
14 M. Shafh et al, *MERU Journal*, 24:29 (1976).
15 Letter to the author dated 25 March 1987.
16 A. James Dix et al, *Journal of Clinical Psychology*, 39:3 (1983).
17 O. Pelletier, *American Journal of Clinical Nutrition*, 23:5 520-524.
18 F. L. Warren, *Biochemistry Journal*. 37:338-341.

Sugar

Sugars are the basic chemical units of all carbohydrates and the most fundamental of all foods. Plants store sugar in their stems and roots to use for energy. Natural sugars are widely distributed in foods, especially honey. fruits and vegetables; carrots also have plenty, as do grapes.

Sugars include glucose, fructose, maltose, lactose and – the one that concerns us most – sucrose.

Since the early 18th century, when we added sugar to our foods for the occasional treat, its use has multiplied about 20 times. Signs are, however, that the sugar boom may have passed its peak. The NACNE (UK National Advisory Committee on Nutrition Education) report, published in 1983, added its voice to the chorus of warnings on sugar, and consumption is dropping. We now get through a mere 40 kilograms or so a year each.

'Impossible' you may think. 'I've given it up in tea and coffee,' but, although you ignore the sugar bowl on the table, and nearly always refuse chocolates, you are eating added sugar every day, not only in cakes and biscuits, but in breakfast cereals, jams, soft drinks, sauces, fruit yoghurts and many 'quick' dinners. Tomato ketchup is 22.9 per cent sugar, dairy ice cream 22.6 per cent, some supermarket muesli 26.2 per cent, sweet pickle 32.6 per cent. There is added sugar in some tinned and frozen vegetables, salad dressings, even packet soups.

Heavily refined sugars are a boon to the food industry. They are extensively used in processing, not only to sweeten, but as activators, preservatives, anti-coagulants, and in fermentation and bulking (i.e. for ice cream). According to the British Sugar Bureau, heavy sucrose syrup gives an 'attractive mouth feel to the product.'

Different kinds of added sugar

The sugars we add to our food come from either sugar beet or cane sugar. They are refined in several stages and this process removes not only dirt and other impurities but the few nutrients that raw, whole sugars boast. Also present in crude sugar cane juice is a factor – destroyed early in refining – which protects the teeth from decay.

First in order of nutritional value comes molasses. The residue from the first sugar crystallization process, molasses is made only from sugar cane. Blackstrap is the least refined. Molasses contains small amounts of vitamins B_1, B_2. pantothenic acid and niacin, with plenty of inositol and B_6. It consists of about 10 per cent minerals – copper, calcium, chromium, phosphorus, magnesium, zinc and plenty of potassium, and also some trace elements. The iron content in blackstrap molasses is more, weight for weight, than in liver; it is one of the best vegetable sources of iron.

Black treacle is thinner and more diluted, and golden syrup and ordinary treacle are much more refined.

Whole, raw muscovado sugar is the first, least refined product of the process which leads in the end to refined white sugar. John Yudkin, the sugar expert, carried out experiments on rats and found that raw, dark muscovado sugar was better food for them than white.

In his book, *The Dictionary of Minerals*[1] (Thorsons, 1985), Dr Leonard Mervyn compares another less refined sugar, raw demerara, with refined white sugar, and this table gives you some idea of nutritional losses as sugar is processed.

Refined white sugar is sold as granulated, castor and icing sugar, sugar cubes and coffee crystals (sometimes dyed).

Look at the label

Sugars are labelled either 'raw' or 'manufactured'. Raw sugars also have the country of origin on the packet. Manufactured sugars are not labelled with their country of origin, and are called 'soft'. They are simply refined white sugars to which molasses or some other caramel colouring has been added. Manufactured sugars are, therefore, more heavily refined and processed than raw varieties.

Minerals in sugar
Minerals (mg per 100g of sugar) in raw demerara and refined white sugar:

	Raw demerara	Refined white sugar
Potassium	89	2
Sodium	6	trace
Calcium	53	2
Magnesium	15	trace
Phosphorus	20	trace
Iron	0.9	trace
Copper	0.06	0.02
Sulphur	14	trace
Chloride	35	trace

Sugar is unnecessary

John Yudkin writes:[2]

If you feel that you must take sugar, then it makes sense to eat brown sugar, provided it really is a good quality raw sugar. You should choose a clean, dark muscovado sugar, which contains the greatest proportion of molasses ... There is no physiological requirement for sugar. All human nutritional needs can be met in full without having to take a single spoon of white or brown or raw sugar, on its own or in any food or drink.

Most practitioners agree with this and find that patients who have trouble coping with refined sugar usually have similar problems with any other kind.

Any kind of sugar which we add to our food is an isolated substance. For our primitive ancestors, the sweetest fruits were the ripest and the most delicious. They ate the fruit as well as the sugar it contained – the whole food, and not a part of it. When we add sugar – dark and raw or refined – to our food now, we are adding something that has been separated from the original sugar cane or sugar beet. (Seven pounds of sugar cane make one pound of sugar, and one huge sugar beet makes about one teaspoonful of sugar.) This is probably one of the reasons some of us cannot tolerate a lot of extra sugar.

Sugar and health

The most obvious effect of too much sugar is that it makes you fat. Obesity starts in the cradle and fat babies make fat people (although breast milk contains no added sugar). We now have more fat children than ever before. They are influenced by junk food advertisements on TV; the annual budget for advertising confectionery alone on British commercial television is well over £20 million.

A diet high in refined sugar (and refined starch) can cause a deficiency of B vitamins, especially vitamin B_1, and the mineral chromium. This is because the body needs these nutrients before it can make use of sugar, and they are absent in refined foods. This may be one reason why people who eat the wrong foods tend to stuff themselves and put on weight. Perhaps the body, craving the many nutrients it is not getting in refined foods, craves vast quantities in the hope of finding nourishment.

It is interesting to note that if you deprive a laboratory rat of vitamin B_1, its appestat – the centre in its brain which tells it when it is hungry or has eaten enough – will cease to work properly. This can lead to either bingeing or starving. Perhaps the appestat in us is also vulnerable to this deficiency.

Sugar and obesity are cause and effect, but less well-known is the link between refined white sugar and behaviour. Sugary foods have been found to worsen behaviour, particularly in hyperactive children.[3] American researcher Stephen J. Schoenthaler found that youths at a detention home who were given a low-sugar diet behaved better and were released sooner than expected.[4]

Further research warned that eating sugary foods from which nutrients have been removed may lower IQ and hamper school achievement.[5]

We may have been too quick to blame the demon cholesterol for the high blood fat levels which accompany heart disease. Volunteers at Queen Elizabeth College, London, piled more sugar into their food and the result was that helpful HDLs (High Density Lipoproteins), which help to carry away excess blood fats, went down. When the volunteers cut their sugar consumption, their blood fat levels went down too.[6] Sugar also encourages a high level of insulin, which damages artery walls.

A strong case has been made for a relationship between sugar and diabetes. When we eat any food, glucose is released from it and passes into the bloodstream, putting up the level of blood sugar. The pancreas releases insulin to lower the blood sugar to normal again. But this natural process is accelerated when we eat sugar. It is absorbed into the bloodstream very quickly and, when we eat a lot of sugar, the pancreas is constantly being asked to produce insulin. This results in a 'trigger-happy' pancreas which can eventually get exhausted and give up. Dr Patrick Pietroni, in his book *Holistic Health*[7] writes that 10 to 15 per cent of the population probably has trouble in dealing with sugar.

> *This means that if their diet is high in simple or refined sugar their bodies respond by secreting a higher level of insulin ... If this continues for a long time, there is good evidence that they will develop diabetes.*

Sugar is one of the factors that encourage a yeast-like organism living in all of us, candida albicans, or thrush, to change its form and cause trouble (other factors are drugs which lower immunity including long-term antibiotics and the Pill). In its changed form, candida can make any food and environmental allergies worse and can precipitate depression, anxiety, mood swings, indigestion, constipation or diarrhoea, lethargy, acne, migraine, cystitis and vaginal infections, and menstrual problems. Giving up all added sugars is an essential part of recovering from thrush.

We all know by now that sugar plays havoc with our teeth. It combines with salivary bacteria to form sticky plaque and this produces an acid which attacks them. This is made easier by a substance, dextran, which forms very readily from white sugar.

Most of our dental problems could be reduced by cutting our intake of sugary foods and refined starches, without recourse to the questionable benefits of fluoride.

In their book *Nutritional Medicine* (Pan Books, 1987),[8] doctors Stephen Davies and Alan Stewart give a gloomy list of the other illnesses they believe are linked with a diet high in white sugar:

- High blood pressure
- Gastro-intestinal disease
- Gallstones
- Kidney stones and kidney failure
- Increased susceptibility to infection

- Depression and anxiety
- Skin problems, including acne, dandruff and eczema
- Low blood sugar
- Allergies.

These last two are intimately involved with the role that sugar plays in addiction.

Sugar addiction

American doctor Abram Hoffer tells the story of a man, not an alcoholic, who was repeatedly thrown into jail because he enjoyed attacking policemen. While he was being questioned, he suddenly began to pour with sweat and pulled two pounds of sugar out of his pocket which he proceeded to wolf down as fast as he could, saying. 'This is the only thing that keeps me well.' He was found to suffer from a sugar addiction, with severe low blood sugar, and was given dietary treatment. The local policemen had no more trouble from him.[9]

But how can we be allergic to sugar, which is not a drug?

The link with low blood sugar

We have seen that sugar can cause a 'trigger-happy' pancreas. As well as being one probable cause of diabetes, these sudden highs and lows associated with refined sugar (and probably with other added sugars as well) can cause low blood sugar, or hypoglycaemia. The sugar load is such that the pancreas releases too much insulin and this clears too much sugar from the blood. So after initial elation and a burst of energy, we feel tired again, and we may suffer from the many other symptoms grouped under the umbrella of low blood sugar.

Most people experience harmless, transient low blood sugar at one time or another; if we are hungry blood sugar falls naturally. The symptoms are very wide and can be difficult to pin down, but basically the most vulnerable part of us when blood sugar drops is the brain. The brain needs the lion's share of the body's available glucose in order to function properly and it has no reserves. So the main symptoms include fatigue, yawning, confusion, trembling, clumsiness, palpitations, anxiety and iritability, sudden ravenous hunger, with high or low emotional states and hot or cold sweats. In other words, almost any transient symptom can be caused by low blood sugar.

When blood sugar plummets the person can undergo a change of personality, even to the extent of beating up policemen; many sufferers have gone the rounds of psychiatrists in vain. It can also make allergies worse, bringing on an attack of asthma or hay fever.

However, this condition is not a disease, but a disturbance in the way the body handles sugar. Even so, the adrenal glands and the liver may become less efficient and, after years of over-reacting and overwork, the pancreas may give up altogether. The result is diabetes.

Since in the first place the person's inability to handle a lot of sugar is one part of his problem (the other is eating too much of an isolated and harmful substance), he has a sugar intolerance, or allergy, as well as a sugar addiction.

Dr Richard Mackarness, the allergy pioneer, wrote[10] that the foods people are most likely to be addicted to are those laden with additives and sugar and 'in my opinion, only heroin or morphine addictions are more potent and destructive than severe food addiction, which I would put on a par with alcoholism.'

Overcoming sugar addiction

Most doctors are not aware that sugar can be an addiction, and the accompanying low blood sugar is considered by many to be 'all in the mind'.

Dr S, however (Directory: 138 Harley Street, W1), uses a wide range of alternative, or complementary, techniques to treat sugar addiction, and searches for reasons why his patients are addicted.

I consider that a healthy person will enjoy normal foods and there will be no desire for drugs or sugar; the system will have no need for them. But when a person is ill – not necessarily in a way you can give a name to, but he is not happy – he is out of balance emotionally, mentally or physically, then he is trying to seek ways and means to overcome that and his addiction will result from the basic dis-ease or discomfort that he is going through.

So we cannot take these things in isolation. We have to look at the total person. What is his make-up? What are the factors that have contributed to his addiction, or craving? I take that approach to any illness and any addiction.

Homoeopathy

Evonne F (Directory: Victoria Road, London NW6) says:

> *Everyone has different nutritional needs; I have never had two patients the same, ever. Diet is a very individual thing. But, if I find that someone has a tremendous sweet tooth, a craving, I can just give them a homoeopathic remedy which will diminish that in a couple of days. They will never eat chocolates on their way to work again.*

Nutrition

Almost all practitioners use this approach. Dr L (Directory: Upper Harley Street, London NW1) treats sugar addiction by treating the low blood sugar which goes with it.

> *Addiction to sugar means that you take on board a lot of refined sugary foods, junk foods, and your pancreas gets used to them. They cause an enormous rush of insulin which knocks the sugar down very quickly and you get low blood sugar. Because this makes you feel slightly shaky, you then feel you need more sugar, say a Mars Bar, and you get into this vicious circle of having to pump up your blood sugar levels, and getting too much insulin, so they drop down again.*
>
> *The primitive diet contained natural foods – unrefined, mixed carbohydrates – which cause a slower rise in blood sugar and insulin output.*
>
> *This very high rise in blood sugar that you get with refined sugary foods, followed by a steep drop because of plenty of insulin is, in my view, a pre-diabetic state.*
>
> *So, with sugar addiction, we tell people to eat small, regular meals of unrefined carbohydrates – wholemeal bread, brown rice, potatoes with their skins and so on – to wean themselves off the sugar gradually. They have to carry an apple in their bag and, when they feel slightly odd, instead of having a bar of chocolate, have the apple, or a carrot.*
>
> *I always explain everything to the patient. Once they understand what is happening inside their own bodies, they can begin to control it, by eating small, regular meals without sugar.*
>
> *We also use homoeopathic remedies for the digestion and herbal remedies for the liver and pancreas. We often see chronic thrush, too, or candida. Candida feeds on sugar and is often associated with*

sugar cravings; it's far more common than people realize.

Naturopath Susan T (Directory: Meopham, Kent) doesn't ask her patients to withdraw from any addiction, even sugar, all at once.

> *I begin always by sorting out a sensible viable routine for the person to live by in the early stages; quite moderate, not extreme.*
>
> *After three months on this regime, when the level of vitality has risen, then we can begin to think about withdrawal. The first step is taking refined sugar, other sugars and honey out of the diet. The second step is taking out any kind of sugar, whether it's supposed to be healthy or not. In that category is dried fruit and many fresh fruits, such as grapes. If there is also a problem with starches, I would then cut out cereals, starting with wheat first. Brown rice is the best. I like to get them on to a good, healthy diet based on salads, some cooked vegetables, some fruits, some meat, fish, nuts and seeds, whole grains – high-quality food with lots of variety.*
>
> *I think it's a problem of sensitivity. If you can get the sugar out of their system, the blood sugar, which has often been a problem, remains beautifully steady.*
>
> *People with a sugar addiction often have weight problems. But if they can get the sugar problem solved, the weight goes down. You can treat obesity this way.*
>
> *People will tend to want more of what their body reacts to; addiction is the same as allergy then.*

Supplements

To treat sugar addiction, it is usually best to attack the underlying low blood sugar, or hypoglycaemia, and this involves giving the patient supplements which will improve the way his body handles sugar.

Zinc is involved in the regulation of insulin release, and chromium works with magnesium and manganese in the handling of sugar, or glucose. Low blood sugar can cause a deficiency of potassium.

The amino acid, tryptophan, has proved effective against depression, and research has now found that blood levels of tryptophan go up after a person has eaten a meal rich in sugars and starches. Volunteers reported feeling more alert and positive after taking tryptophan.

Perhaps, therefore, someone eating a lot of sugar and starch is simply trying to lift their feeling of depression in this way. In the *Journal of Alternative and Complementary Medicine*[11] naturopath Leon Chaitow writes:

> A supplementation with tryptophan could replace the effects of carbohydrate craving and play a large part in maintaining adherence to diet.

The amino acid glutamine can, for some people, decrease their desire for sugar.[12] The reason for this may be that it acts on the appestat, the centre in the brain which controls our appetite.

If you wish to use amino acid therapy, please consult a practitioner who understands it.

A case history: Ann

'I had had migraines every few weeks for ten years. I was having gastric flu with diarrhoea every couple of months which made me very sick. I couldn't sleep and found it terribly hard to get up in the morning, and – together with my sugar cravings – I was overweight – 11 stone 9 lbs.

'I had been to my doctor yet again and had an appointment to see a gastro-enterologist, but I didn't go because by that time I was having dietary therapy, with Pat (Directory: Brandlehow Road, London SW15). I went to her because I thought my troubles were very likely to do with diet, and I certainly didn't want to take drugs.

'First of all she took a lengthy case history, a couple of hours, and then she diagnosed sugar addiction and low blood sugar (hypoglycaemia). At home, we had given up sugar in tea and coffee, but we were still having jams, marmalade, honey, and I made cakes and biscuits for the children using brown sugar. We had been using sugar in savoury foods, too; putting sugar in salad dressing, sugar in meat meals. There are many recipes, particularly American, that recommend adding sugar to casseroles and so forth. So although we tended not to eat sweets, sugar was creeping in to all our foods.

'Pat put me on a diet, or rather, a way of eating. It wasn't one of those crash diets which made you lose weight very quickly and then you put it all back again. She explained it to me and I could see the point of it. I found it very helpful.

'It cut out all sugars – honey, jam, marmalade, added sugars, and dairy foods. I was allowed lots of natural yoghurt, though. I didn't drink much coffee, tea or alcohol. I have tried to cut these down but I haven't cut them out completely, in fact. I ate lots of brown rice. Pat explained that it absorbs toxins from the digestive system. I wasn't allowed beef or pork; it turned out that I had several food intolerances besides sugar, and the beef was responsible for the gastric 'flu episodes. Red wine was causing the migraines, so I cut this out too. I ate lots of fruit, salads and vegetables and drank juices and water.

'I took quite a lot of supplements; the whole range of B vitamins, especially pantothenic acid, with vitamins A and D; calcium, magnesium, lecithin and acidophilus (a digestive supplement).

'By about July I noticed a great improvement. I had lost a stone in weight, the migraines had disappeared, and the gastric 'flu has never come back either. I felt a lot more energetic, too.

'I am now (October 1987) much better, but not completely well. Although all my symptoms have gone, I still find it difficult sometimes to sleep and get up in the morning afterwards, but not often. I now weigh 10 stone 4 lbs. I have breakfast, lunch and supper and if I am hungry I might have some crunchy grains or fruit in between. I do find it hard to keep to the diet strictly, however. There are times when I have lapsed, particularly on holiday. I don't want to sound incredibly strong-willed.

'I do lead quite an exhausting life, and I cope very well. I have a full-time job, a family to look after, and political work in the evenings. I still see Pat, but only once every couple of months. I feel, altogether, very energetic and much better.'

Sugar cravings: helping yourself

The typical sugar (or other refined carbohydrates) addict will probably not want breakfast, making do with a cup of sweet coffee and perhaps a cigarette (and maybe a nibble of chocolate on the way to work). He or she gets ravenously hungry for sugary foods during the day and may sip sweet coffee or tea throughout to keep going. A large evening meal – by this time he's weak from hunger – will simply put weight on (which doesn't happen if most of the calories are taken early in the day).

This way of eating not only makes you fat, it makes you ill as well.

Getting over your sugar cravings entails re-educating your body out of the highs and lows of hypoglycaemia. Please remember that too much tea and coffee can cause the blood sugar to see-saw, as can a cigarette, and that sugar on its own is quicker to enter the bloodstream than sugar eaten with a meal. Other causes of hypoglycaemic reaction with a craving for sugar are severe dieting, fasting on water only, continued stress and numerous drugs; analgesics including aspirin, anti-inflammatory drugs, anti-coagulants, antibiotics, diuretics, stimulants, tranquillizers and hormones including the Pill.

From the dietary approach which the practitioners have described you will see that you should eventually cut all added sugars out of your diet. However, you may experience withdrawal symptoms if you stop sugar abruptly, so it's better to tail it off gradually. It has been giving you a temporary 'kick', so your body needs time to adjust to a calmer, more natural rhythm without it.

Raw fruits, salads and briefly-cooked vegetables contain fibre which helps to stabilize blood sugar levels and cut down hypoglycaemia, and you may find that you can cope with their natural sugars.

Don't let yourself get hungry. Take small meals, and if you are hungry take a small snack, such as crispbread and cottage cheese, a glass of milk or some yoghurt, or some nuts, seeds, and dried or fresh fruit. If you take fruit or vegetable juices, always have some food as well.

You may find it necessary to consult a qualified practitioner who has had experience in treating low blood sugar problems for specific advice.

Please remember that the sugar we add to our foods is not necessary to health, and that applies to brown sugar as well as white. There are natural sugars in the fruits and vegetables we eat, and starches such as cereals and starchy vegetables are changed into natural sugars during digestion. Even meat contains some starch, which is turned into sugars by the body.

In fact, about 65 per cent of the food we put into our mouths is turned into sugars – a full quota for anyone, without ever going near a sugar bowl.

Please see the directory for more information.

References

1 *The Dictionary of Minerals*, Leonard Mervyn (Thorsons, 1985).

2 *Pure, White and Deadly*, John Yudkin (Viking, 1986).
3 D. S. King, *Nutrition and Health*, 3:3.
4 *Society of Environmental Therapy Newletter*, 2:3.
5 M. and L. Colgan, *Nutrition and Health*, 3:1/2.
6 *Journal of Alternative Medicine*, March 1987.
7 *Holistic Living*, Dr Patrick Pietroni (Dent, 1986).
8 *Nutritional Medicine*, Dr Stephen Davies and Dr Alan Stewart (Pan Books, 1987).
9 *Diet, Crime and Delinquency*, Alexander Schauss (Parker House, 1981).
10 *Not All in the Mind*, Dr Richard Mackarness (Pan Books, 1978).
11 *Journal of Alternative and Complementary Medicine*, June 1987.
12 *Amino Acids in Therapy*, Leon Chaitow (Thorsons, 1985).

Tranquillizers

The drugs I am writing about here are the three most commonly prescibed minor tranquillizers, a group called the benzodiazepines. Previously available as Valium, Librium and Ativan, they can now be prescribed under the NHS as diazepam (brand-name equivalent Valium), chlordiazepoxide (Librium) and lorazepam (Ativan). These generic drugs contain the same active ingredients as do the corresponding brand names, but they are not necessarily identical. The bestseller among them is diazepam, or Valium.

The benzodiazepines were first introduced in the early 1960s, when they were found effective in calming wild animals. At that time, two or three people a day were dying from deliberate barbiturate overdose, and the benzodiazepines were hailed as a safe, non-addictive alternative.

At first, they were prescribed for a wide range of conditions, including allergies and high blood pressure, but they soon cornered the market in emotional problems: bereavement, loneliness, divorce or an unhappy marriage, money or job worries, anxiety and chronic tension. Within a few years they were the most widely prescribed drugs in the world.

Promoted through expensive and skilful publicity campaigns aimed at the medical profession, they were given, not only for the real crises in life, but as part of the philosophy 'a pill for every ill' – the idea that medicine should deal with, and suppress, reactions to the ordinary anxieties, confusions and uncertainties that are an inescapable part of being vulnerable and being alive.

Doctors, not trained to help with their patients' worries, came to believe that a prescription for tranquillizers was useful and safe. Nobody knew that these drugs were addictive. Within a few years repeat prescriptions without consultation were so widespread that as many as 90 per cent were written this way. Hospital patients would be given the drugs as a matter of routine to help them sleep, and discharged with more pills; GPs would sometimes continue prescribing them simply because they appeared on the hospital record.

Now, because of warnings from the media and because of doctors' concerns, patients are taking fewer of these potentially addictive and damaging drugs. Even so, the DHSS states that over 25 million prescriptions for benzodiazepines were issued in 1985 and it is estimated that about half a million people in the UK are addicted to tranquillizers.

Effects

There is nothing minor about the minor tranquillizers. Most are long-acting drugs (although Ativan is shorter-acting). They act quickly on the central nervous system and brain, changing neurotransmitters, decreasing the level of consciousness and relieving anxiety and tension; even awareness of colours, sounds and other sense impressions can be blurred. They damp down all bodily functions, relaxing tense muscles (and are therefore valuable for epilepsy). Eventually, they enter every body cell.

But, although they work well at first, no benzodiazepine is effective for longer than a matter of weeks.[1] After four months' continuous use, you can get addicted, and the effects of benzodiazepine addiction are both physical and psychological and extremely severe.

Physical effects after long-term use include fatigue, digestive upsets and aches and pains, with feelings of general ill-health. Users can have dull eyes, muddy skin and lank hair.

The drugs can damage the liver.[2] They can cause hormonal imbalances so that men develop swollen breasts and painful testicles, impotence, acne and loss of seminal fluid. Women may have heavy menstrual bleeding,[3] and may experience a fall in sexual desire.

Pregnant women should not take benzodiazepines. There is also a danger that babies might be influenced by the drugs, which can get into breast milk.[4] They may also encourage cancer, but there is at present no definite proof.

Long-term use can cause brain damage. Malcolm Lader,

Professor of Psychopharmacology at the Institute of Psychiatry in London, carried out brain scans on 20 patients who had been taking Valium for between five and ten years. Five had normal scans, ten showed serious changes suggesting impairment, and the remaining five showed marked abnormalities, including brain shrinkage and loss of neural function.[5] Scandinavian research found that if a patient takes Valium he probably won't be able to recall anything he learned while on the drug *unless he starts taking it again*. In elderly people, whose livers and kidneys are less able to dispose of drugs and their toxins effectively, long-term use can cause drowsiness, poor co-ordination and impaired judgement. A study carried out by Professor Doll at Oxford University covering over 40,000 people found a link, confirmed by several other studies, between benzodiazepines and road accidents.[6]

So these drugs affect your ability to think and react, as well as your enjoyment of life.

By lifting inhibitions in people who are usually uptight, benzodiazepines may in fact allow them to be more hostile and aggressive. This may even contribute towards the increased incidence of baby battering. A report in the *American Journal of Psychiatry*, confirmed by several others, states that they can actually *cause* anxiety and depression. Research published in the *Journal of the American Medical Association*, found that, of eight patients on a normal dose of Valium, seven thought of suicide, four of those tried it, and two succeeded. Five out of the six patients still surviving felt better a few days after stopping the drug.

Suspicions that the drugs might be ineffective were raised by Medical Research Council trials reported in the *Daily Mail* on 25 January 1979. Valium was no more effective than no drugs at all for most of 240 patients with anxiety and depression.

Finally, benzodiazepines don't mix with other drugs, including alcohol; the resulting cocktail can be dangerous. Many people on tranquillizers also drink plenty of coffee to perk themselves up and, when the caffeine makes them feel nervous, take another pill to calm themselves down again.

Withdrawals and coming off

Not everybody suffers withdrawal symptoms, but the longer you have been taking the drug and the higher the dosage, the more likely you are to have problems giving up. For those who do stop, these drugs can be harder to come off after long-term use than heroin (Ativan is considered by many practitioners to be the worst). *Suddenly stopping is extemely dangerous.*

Symptoms usually start two to three days after you have stopped. In some people they can persist for several months and the body may not be finally clean of the drugs for up to two years. But, however awful withdrawals are, they do disappear in the end.

Here is a list of the *possible* withdrawal symptoms:

- A strong craving for the drug
- Trembling, dizziness, feeling separate from your body and disorientated
- Insomnia and fatigue
- Nausea, metallic taste in the mouth, sore tongue, stomach pains
- Overbreathing (hyperventilation)
- Headaches
- Weight loss
- Palpitations or slow pulse, changes in blood pressure
- 'Flu-like feelings
- Increased sensitivity to light, noise, touch and smell
- Hot and cold feelings; creeping sensation on skin; sweats
- Aching muscles; pain in jaw
- Blurred speech, blurred vision
- Tightness in chest
- Fits (only on stopping abruptly)
- Great anxiety and fear; depression
- Sudden rages
- Mental confusion; inability to concentrate
- Hallucinations
- Resurgence of old grief and pain, buried when you started taking the drug.

Do not try to come off quickly. If your practitioner advises you to do this, find another practitioner who understands the subject better. You may need support from people who have been through withdrawals themselves; please see the information section for groups of people who can help you.

As a rough guide, Professor Malcolm Lader recommends cutting down the commonest tranquillizer, diazepam (Valium), for rapid withdrawal in this way: reduce a total dose of, say, 15 mg a day to a total of 12 mg a day for the first week, then to a total of 9 mg a day for the second week, 6 mg a day for the third week and 3 mg a day for the fourth, and so on. This is for people who are fit and have not been long-term users.[3] He does not consider it safe to withdraw any faster than this.

Orthodox ways of cutting down

Many people are able to come off their pills successfully with their doctor's help by simply cutting them down gradually. Some doctors replace the shorter-acting lorazepam (Ativan) with diazepam (Valium). Some give intermittent doses of propranolol (propranolol hydrochloride, or Inderal), a heart drug, useful as a mild sedative. However, Ativan is more difficult to withdraw from than Valium and propranolol can have unpleasant side-effects, including nausea, vomiting and diarrhoea.

A doctor may arrange for long-term users to withdraw in hospital, where they can relax in safe, supportive surroundings.

The danger with this kind of treatment is that the patient may find that he or she has replaced one addiction with another.

Drugless treatments for tranquillizer addiction

Most of the practitioners I spoke to have an extensive experience in treating tranquillizer dependence.

Acupuncture

Acupuncturist Caroline K (Directory: Barbican, London EC2) condemns the tranquillizer boom.

The way these drugs have been handed out in the past on prescription is almost criminal. I sometimes have patients who have been on tranquillizers since their teens, for 10 or 15 years. By this time it is very difficult to withdraw them and so, even using acupuncture as well. I cut them down terribly, terribly slowly. You don't take risks with people whose systems have been heavily dependent on these drugs. How fast varies; I don't have any standard rate. I look at what they are taking, how long they have been on it, and work out with them how fast they are going to come off. I adjust it carefully by how the individual is coping with the reduction, and I always make sure that they have their doctor's agreement.

During withdrawal, some people get feelings of malaise. They may be low in energy and feel anxious, with palpitations and insomnia. If they took the pills for some grief or problem, when they come off, it will still be there, unresolved or unexpressed. I find that listening to people's problems is a very important part of what I do. It's definitely part of the treatment.

Garnett S (Directory: Woodhouse Road, London N12) agrees that grief and conflict lie dormant until the drug is given up.

You're not allowing the patient who takes them to help themselves or to grieve. Everything is getting locked up. Take back pain, for instance. There's a difference between the sexes there. When a man gets back pain he'll get aggressive because he can't get out and move. But when a woman gets back pain, she'll get depressed, and her GP will give her tranquillizers for her depression. So a lot of women with back pain end up taking tranquillizers . . .

The Chinese doctors say that you get your energy from two sources – the air you breathe and the food you eat. So I try to get people to do breathing exercises and go for walks, and I use nutrition. Some people are quite keen to work with their diets, but unfortunately, some are indifferent. For those who are interested, I give vitamin C, B-complex, and a multi-mineral supplement. Calcium is especially good. Often the reason people can't sleep is that they are simply short of calcium. Sometimes I use tryptophan (an amino acid) as well. It helps if they are depressed and also helps with sleeping.

Herbalism

Julian B (Directory: Wilbury Road, Hove, Sussex) is another practitioner trying to cope with the tranquillizer epidemic.

I treat tranquillizers, mostly. Sometimes a person's problem has started 30 years ago. One lady of about 80 I'm treating has problems which started in her early twenties. Another patient who is reducing her dose has a long history of being in and out of psychiatric hospitals. I take a different approach with different people. You won't get anywhere with a formula you just apply to everybody; you might as well prescribe Valium. I suppose, in listening to people, I am playing a lost role. The country doctor used to do it, I imagine, or the parish priest. I find that an hour-and-a-half's consultation enables the patient to get another perspective as they talk about the problem.

I'm always happy to work with the doctor, but first of all I make sure what the patients want. If they say, 'I'm determined to come off the pills,' then that's a fair brief. If they are not sure yet, I don't think it's my job to pressurize them. Some don't want to come off completely because they are insecure. If you can make them feel more secure, they arrive at a point where they are ready to come off. You do find the same herbs coming up again and again in prescribing for this, but nonetheless they are not formulated. One doesn't just take a bottle of something off the shelf and hand it to the patient as though it is an orthodox drug; each person has their own individual prescription.

In an article published in the *Journal of Alternative Medicine* in April 1985, David Hoffman stresses the holistic approach during withdrawal.

The whole process can be speeded up safely by using herbal remedies at the same time. Not only will this reduce withdrawal symptoms, more importantly it will tone and strengthen the nervous system after its exposure to intense chemical stress (paradoxically meant to relieve the psychological impact of life stress!). It cannot be stressed enough that the aim is to help the person come off drugs and the need for an artificial psychological support, not to replace benzodiazepines with herbal nervines.

He has found that the patient needs constant reassurance and explanation while he weathers this phase, as well as help with understanding his emotional reactions as he sorts out his emerging feelings. A herbal prescription, drawn up to suit the individual patient, is used to:

. . . gently relax somatic and psychological tensions, thus allowing the body and mind to regain a natural 'nervous tone'. This approach is based on the view that the innate healing mechanisms of the body will do what is necessary, given the chance. The herbs will give this chance.

Herbal medicine does not usually work quickly. John H (Directory: London Road, Leicester) says:

It is a long process, and at all stages, the operative word is 'gradual'. Treatment has to be individually prescribed, very carefully monitored, and there must be regular consultations for support and counselling. Treatment is aimed at building up and feeding the patient's nervous system so that ultimately a gradual withdrawal of the hitherto needed drug can be done without any side-effects.

Hypnotherapy

Alastair B (Directory: 31, Harley Street, London W1) says:

I see an awful lot of people who have been on tranquillizers for a hell of a long time. Many people who come here have been on them for 20 years. At that stage, I'm not going to try and get them off straightaway. Getting people off these prescribed drugs is more difficult than getting them off heroin. It's absolutely horrifying. You can go straight into hypnoanalysis under tranquillizers, but you probably won't have a successful outcome because they change the way you think and feel too much. You have probably surrendered all charge of yourself over the time you have been taking these drugs. You are no longer in the driving seat.

John B (Directory: Halford Road, London SW6) also uses a very careful, gradual approach, and finds that his patient's dependence lessens as his or her condition improves. He looks for the reasons why the person took the drug in the first place.

Treatment for tranquillizer addiction is usually undertaken as part of the ongoing treatment of anxiety neurosis, stress and tension conditions and other types of nervous problems, for which tranquillizers are usually prescribed.

Antonia C (Directory: Rochester Square, London NW1) helps her patients to face up to the original problems which led them to use tranquillizers.

One of the main reasons people take tranquillizers is to help anxiety states, panic attacks, things like that. Usually, when a panic attack happens to an adult, it is not in fact the first time. They were usually sensitized in childhood. For instance, perhaps they get a panic attack in a lift and they develop claustrophobia. Though these attacks may only have started a few years ago as far as they are consciously aware, there is usually an episode in childhood that precipitated them. Having gone back to the childhood experience under hypnosis, they can be helped to see it again and put it in a different perspective. You take the understanding of the adult back to the child, and relieve the child and give it resources it didn't have before, which helps the adult. When cutting the dose, I usually work with the doctor, and I get clients to use self-hypnosis for any addiction, between sessions with me, and I make a tape for them too. If a person has had to go on tranquillizers it usually means that they are sensitive and very prone to stress. If you are like this, then you do need to monitor your stress levels all the time, and use relaxation, every day.

Australian researchers found that hypnotherapy, together with supplements, succeeded in helping two patients to withdraw from tranquillizers.[7]

Nutrition

Tuula T (Directory: Pixham Lane, Dorking, Surrey) uses nutrition with a wide range of supplements. She stresses that tranquillizers can actually cause nutritional deficiencies, and that the body needs several vitamins and minerals in order to get rid of their toxic effects.

She also states that all addictions bring with them the tendency to low blood sugar, or hypoglycaemia, with its sudden swings between energy and fatigue, and that this must be treated nutritionally.

She uses vitamin C, several B vitamins and minerals, the amino acid L-glutamine and gamma linolenic acid (found in evening primrose oil), and puts her patients on a wholefood diet with a good protein breakfast. Tobacco, alcohol, coffee and strong tea must be cut out, and if low blood sugar is marked, small protein-based snacks taken every three hours or so.

Most practitioners include nutritional advice in their treatment.

Osteopathy and cranial osteopathy

Susan T (Directory: Birtrick Drive, Meopham, Kent) has treated many people who were addicted to tranquillizers.

The 'something to help' has rapidly become addictive. It takes less than a week in some cases, and confirms the patient's attitude that, on his own, he cannot cope with life. He cannot sleep without his Mogadon and he can't face the day without his Valium. Shame and rebellion against this monstrous regime, a desire to take charge of his life again, may precipitate a violent withdrawal syndrome that usually results in resigned or frustrated acceptance of more prescriptions.

My approach asks for the patient's complete commitment over a long period. It's also useful to work out a 'lifestyle routine' with most patients, one designed to improve their general health, with good nutrition, exercise and deep breathing, and time taken for leisure. Most essential is a period of deliberate relaxation for half an hour daily. Occasionally the Bach flower remedies can help.

Osteopathy can have a direct influence on how energetic a person feels.

What is common to all these patients is the lack of responsiveness and energy. Vitality is poor, it's working against the odds all the time. No wonder patient morale is so low at first. Gradually, with osteopathy and cranial work too, the person gains in strength, flexibility and rhythm.

Patients may bottle up the reasons why they took the drug in the first place, reasons which will be expressed in tensions or body armouring.

I treat these tensions osteopathically and I listen to their problems with as much sympathy and objectivity as I can, obeying our osteopathic rule of minimal interference, and letting the person work it out for himself even if it means letting him make his own mistakes.

She warns about the dangers of coming off too quickly:

Coping with drug withdrawal is like lifting the lid from a boiling saucepan. Take it off too quickly and the escaping steam burns. So if we abruptly stop the drug, we provoke a violent body response. It is better to lift the lid very gently and control the rate and intensity of withdrawal effects. I work once a week, sometimes for six months with some patients. There comes a point when, with the good diet and all the other good things you have asked them to do, there is a breakthrough — you feel more vitality. At that point, and at that point only, do I ask them to start withdrawing.

There is often intense discomfort during every phase, but if patients understand that every time they get the jitters, palpitations, blinding headaches, this is the body trying to cleanse itself, then they have a totally different attitude to somebody who just feels grotty all the time and doesn't understand why. They realize that their symptoms show the body's increasing vitality and their attitude to the withdrawal process is transformed.

Transcendental Meditation

Roger L (Directory: Transcendental Meditation) says:

We teach TM to a lot of people who are referred by doctors and psychiatrists because they don't want to go on taking sedatives, and a lot come by themselves. We are very careful about how we deal with the situation. We get people saying, 'I'm starting to meditate now so I'll come off my tranquillizers.' We had one woman who had been on them for ten years and gave them up all at once, and she wondered why after two or three days she didn't feel so good. She was having withdrawal symptoms. We warn them very carefully; people can get over-enthusiastic. We always work in close communication with the doctor or the psychiatrist and they reduce the pills gradually.

We find that usually in a couple of months people can stop. Generally, people find with meditation that there is no need for sedatives and tranquillizers any more. But it varies; some people who are very anxious and depressed can take longer and they will need a lot of support from the teacher. Results are good; the research shows that.

Studies of people taking various drugs, including tranquillizers, show that TM helps cut down on drug use.[8]

A case history: Peggy

It all started nine years ago. My father died suddenly and the shock of it never really came out; I didn't cry at all. Then, after a severe asthma attack, I had a cardiac arrest, and after that my nerves just shattered.

'The doctors just gave me Ativan. They said, "you can't get addicted," but of course, I realize now that you can. I had the Ativan for a total of about eight years.

'After I had been taking it for about two years, I was in the middle of town and I had a panic attack. I felt hot, cold, I was shaking and felt like collapsing. They just gave me stronger Ativan and told me to up the dose if I needed to.

'I found it didn't help very much. I started to get agoraphobia; I didn't want to go out. Things went from bad to worse and I just went to pieces. I had to give up my job. I was just nervous of everything and everybody. I couldn't go out at all in the end.

'I first had herbal treatment in November 1985 because a friend had recommended it, and my husband took me in the car to see the medical herbalist. She examined me very thoroughly and went into everything that had happened and gave me several tests and some medicine.

'The day after I just shook all day and there were no signs of feeling any better so I gave it up; I chucked it down the loo. I thought, "It's not going to work." Nobody had told me that herbal medicine takes time.

'By January of the next year, I was desperate. I couldn't eat, I couldn't sleep or do anything. I couldn't walk out of the door. By then I must have been addicted to Ativan.

'I went back to the herbalist, in a terrible state. She told me not to panic; I was one of thousands. She gave me some more herbal medicine. She told me to cut the Ativan down, very slowly indeed, under her guidance.

'My state then went slowly from very bad to very much better. Over about ten months I got completely better.

'While I took the herbal medicine, I noticed that I could sleep again, relax again. I started to feel normal for the first time in years.

'The herbal treatment is finished now; I haven't had any for ten months. And I haven't had any Ativan for nearly a year.

'I can go out on my own now, I drive the car and I have applied for another job. Without the herbal treatment I couldn't have left the house.

'The doctors couldn't help me with my nervous troubles; they just gave me pills and more pills. They didn't ever get to the root of the problem. But my herbalist has time to sit and listen to me, and I could always just pick up the 'phone and call her.

'The only thing I find a problem with alternative medicine is the cost; it is expensive. But you can't put a price on health.

'My life is happier now than it's been for a long time.'

Please see the directory for more information.

References

1 Committee on Review of Medicines. Quoted in *The Tranquillizer Trap*, Joy Melville (Fontana, 1984).

2 F. J. Tedesco et al, *Digestive Diseases and Science*, May 1982.
3 *Coming off Tranquillizers*, Shirley Trickett (Thorsons, 1986).
4 *Drugs and Therapeutics Bulletin*, January 1983.
5 The *Observer*, 18 April 1982.
6 *Life Without Tranquillizers*, Dr Vernon Coleman (Piatkus, 1985).
7 D. R. Collinson, *Australian Journal of Clinical and Experimental Hypnosis*, 13: 1 (1985).
8 A. and E. N. Aron, *Addictive Behaviours*, 5 (1980).

Part Two
Remedies

Acupuncture

Acupuncture is believed to go back about 5,000 years. The first known text on the subject is the Yellow Emperor's *Classic of Internal Medicine*, or the *Nei Ching Su Wen*. If he existed, the Yellow Emperor probably lived between 2600 and 2700 BC.

The Nei Ching gives the philosophy of Chinese medicine. To the Chinese doctor, disease is of the whole person and represents a lack of harmony with universal principles, a failure to follow Tao in the right way. Acupuncture is just one aspect of traditional Chinese medicine, which also includes herbal treatment, exercise, massage and diet.

By the time of the Ming dynasty, spanning the 14th to the 17th centuries, acupuncture had developed fast and several other textbooks had appeared.

In the early 16th century, the Portuguese landed at Macao and Europe looked to China. Medical missionaries began to swarm into the continent. But their limited skill and crude surgery were regarded with horror by the Chinese. Confucianism held that the body is sacred, both in life and death, and that it is important to meet one's ancestors intact.

Western ideas continued to spread, however, and by 1822 acupuncture had been struck off the curriculum of the Imperial Medical College, to be finally outlawed in 1929.

Acupuncture was alternately reinstated and banned during the power battles of the 1950s onwards and now it is both widely researched and used throughout China. It is an integral part of medical practice, used by both physicians and 'barefoot doctors' – paramedics who have taken a shorter training. The Chinese combine their traditional medical skills with surgery and Western drugs.

Acupuncture is practised in several other Oriental countries, including Vietnam and Japan, and in Sri Lanka it is part of the national health service.

French Jesuit priests brought back some knowledge of acupuncture to Europe during the 17th century. It was not widely known in England until the 1960s, when Dr Felix Mann studied and wrote about it extensively.

In the early 1970s, a team of American doctors visited China and watched surgical operations. Professor Samuel Rosen of the Mount Sinai School of Medicine wrote:

It is an extraordinary experience to see a patient lying relaxed and awake, sipping tea, on an operating table, an acupuncturist twirling a needle about two inches long above her wrist, while a tubercular lung is removed.

Acupuncture is now widely practised in the West and in Russia. In the UK, there are about 1,000 acupuncturists, including both lay practitioners and doctors who have studied it.

Theory and practice

The theory behind Chinese acupuncture is extremely complex. Some practitioners believe it could with benefit be simplified. It is a radically different approach from that of modern orthodox medicine. Tao, literally, 'the Way', is an idea which lies behind all traditional Chinese medicine. It represents the harmony between man and his world, and between this world and beyond. This harmony is a state of balance, the extremes of which are called Yin and Yang. These two polarities are linked and need each other; life is constantly swinging between them. Broadly speaking, Yang represents masculinity – the positive, open qualities – and Yin is the feminine side, negative, quiet and still. The body is a balance of Yang and Yin and this balance is constantly shifting. Acupuncture tries to correct any excessive imbalance between these qualities.

The Ch'i of a person is his total vital force, his flow of energy. It is carried round the body in channels known as meridians, which pass through the acupuncture points. (Some meridians and points are identified with the Five Elements and are named fire, earth, water, metal and wood; these are not actual elements, but symbols.) The acupuncture points link up with different organs of the body. By treating these points with needles, acupuncture tries to correct both the disturbance in the flow of Ch'i which accompanies illness, and the illness itself.

Thus acupuncture works in a very subtle way and, because it can correct a slight imbalance in a person's health, it can stop latent illness from developing any further. The traditional Chinese physician was encouraged to treat his patients to keep them well, not wait until they were obviously ill.

Some traditional acupuncturists take a patient's pulse or look at his tongue for help in diagnosis. Acupuncture pulse-taking is quite different from that of a Western doctor. It tests six pulse points on each wrist, all linked with body organs. From the qualities of each pulse the acupuncturist can tell which organ is diseased and where the Ch'i is not flowing as it should.

There are about 1,000 acupuncture points, 300 of which are commonly used. Modern acupuncture needles are inserted just into the surface of the skin, without drawing blood and usually without causing pain.

Sometimes moxibustion is used too. A small cone of dried leaves is put onto the acupuncture point, lit at the top and lifted quickly off before it can burn down far enough to reach the skin.

Massage, another technique, includes acupressure, which uses fingers, knuckles and even elbows.

Ear acupuncture, or auriculotherapy, is a separate approach which developed outside China. It was known to Hippocrates, and instruments for treating ear points were found in the Egyptian pyramids. Now, the Chinese are skilled in this approach too. They say that all organs of the body are linked to, and represented by, points on the ear and that there are acupuncture charts of the body on the hands, feet and even the face as well.

Many modern acupuncturists use electrical stimulators producing small-amplitude pulsed currents instead of needles. This marriage of an ancient therapy with modern technology is highly effective and becoming widely used.

Most research into acupuncture explores its effects on pain, especially during surgical operations. Acupuncture takes away some or all of the pain but leaves the patient conscious, so it is an analgesic, not an anaesthetic. But it does not work for everyone. Reported percentages of patients able to undergo surgery with acupuncture as the only method of pain relief vary widely from about 10 per cent[1] to 97.7 per cent.[2]

Involved in the natural relief of pain is a group of hormones called the endorphins, and acupuncture can stimulate the body to release them. But this does not explain acupuncture analgesia entirely since, although it can relieve painful conditions almost at once, endorphins only reach a working level in the spinal fluid after 20 minutes of needling.

Another theory – that acupuncture can close a hypothetical 'gate' of nerve fibres in the spinal cord which admits pain signals to the brain – is not really satisfactory either. The pain-relieving effects of acupuncture can persist after treatment for far longer than the gate would remain open.

In any case (and contrary to what many orthodox doctors believe) pain relief is only one of acupuncture's functions; research has proved its value in a wide range of conditions.

Acupuncture can normalize heartbeat, correct high or low blood pressure, and increase the efficiency of the immune system.[3] It has proved effective against headaches,[4] including migraine,[5] and ear acupuncture has reduced overweight.[6] A Chinese study over ten years found it it cured about one-third of 168 cases of squint.[7]

The following is condensed from a provisional list drawn up by the World Health Organization of the uses of acupuncture.

Some respiratory conditions (bronchitis, asthma, etc.)
Some gastro-intestinal disorders (colitis, gastritis, ulcer, etc.)
Some eye, dental and throat disorders (conjunctivitis, gingivitis, sore throat etc.)
Some neurological and musculo-skeletal disorders (migraine, neuralgia, stroke, sciatica, bed-wetting, frozen shoulder and tennis elbow, osteoarthritis, sprains, etc.)

Acupuncture can help angina, pain during childbirth and some ear and skin conditions. Psychological disorders successfully treated include depression and anxiety. It is often used now for treating drug addiction and can reduce the withdrawal symptoms from alcohol, nicotine, narcotics, tranquillizers and heroin.

Please bear in mind that, for some people, acupuncture does not work so it will not be the right approach.

Risks

Most doctors who use acupuncture have taken short courses which only teach its pain-relieving effects. But traditional acupuncturists say that these courses – some of which only last a weekend – are insufficient and produce 'cowboy' acupuncturists who, by indiscriminately using points without enough knowledge, can cause further illness.

Needles must be sterilized, particularly staples or press needles left in the ear. However, the warning put out by the British Medical Association's working party on alternative medicine, that needles could carry AIDS, is completely hypothetical and without any supporting evidence. 'The attempt by the BMA to link acupuncture with infectious diseases is without foundation and scurrilous.'[8]

Please turn to the directory for information on where to find a qualified practitioner.

References

1 *Acupuncture*, Dr Alexander Macdonald (Allen and Unwin, 1982).
2 The Shanghai Acupuncture Anaesthesia Co-ordinating Group, reported in the *Chinese Medical Journal*, January, 1975.
3 The Peking Acupuncture Anaesthesia Co-ordinating Group, reported in *Acupuncture Anaesthesia* (Foreign Language Press, 1972).
4 *Natural Medicine*, July 1986.
5 *American Journal of Acupuncture*, 14: 2, April 1986.
6 *Traditional Chinese Medicine*, 55: 2, pp 87–88.
7 *Journal of Traditional Chinese Medicine*, 4: 3, 1984.
8 The Council for Acupuncture, reported in the *Journal of Alternative Medicine*, August 1986.

Counselling and psychotherapy

We have all been counsellors. We have all listened to someone's troubles and responded sympathetically. By showing understanding and by not judging, we can help an unhappy person feel more positive and clear-headed about his or her problems. We all know that a trouble shared is a trouble halved.

But the disappearance of the large, close-knit family, with strong, permanent local ties, means that the amateur – and often very skilled – counselling given by older people has had to be replaced by that given by people who are strangers, both to the client and to his life. This is one reason why modern professional counselling demands commitment to a course of training.

Much of the time given by social workers, clergymen and doctors is taken up with counselling; it is estimated that between a third and a half of those consulting their doctors have emotional problems, and many doctors have recognized the need for additional training to meet this need.

Counselling can make the difference between hope and despair for some and, by helping them to see things differently, can give the extra push needed at a time of perhaps almost unbearable crisis. Or it can help someone look at, and change that part of him which is distorting his life.

Psychotherapy is a more complex process. In its attempts to illuminate and unravel the client's problems, it can go more deeply into his psychology and history. Although it has grown out of the work pioneered by Freud and Jung, it is less structured than classical psychoanalysis.

Broadly speaking, both counselling and psychotherapy, which often overlap or are indistinguishable, try to help a person sor himself out so that he feels happy with himself, at ease with his fellows, and able to give and receive affection in a healthy way. He moves towards coping effectively with his life and, above all, accepting himself, with all his scars and shortcomings, honestly and lovingly.

Clients range from competent people who need help with a temporary impasse, to the long-term mentally ill (usually treated by a psychotherapist). Both counselling and psychotherapy are used with individuals, families and other groups, including those sharing the problems of addiction.

The field is crowded with different theories and schools, but they all share the beliefs that people are capable of growth and change, and that they need, and are able to help, each other.

Change depends on the client being able to see, with the help of his therapist, but primarily for himself, what has gone wrong and why. This sorting out and confrontation are not simply cool intellectual feats, but can involve a lot of painful digging into the past (more likely in psychotherapy) and the cathartic release of buried emotions. This 'facing up', done with skilled and sympathetic support, can arm him with the insight and self-confidence to recover from his wounds and initiate profound changes in attitude which can alter his whole life.

All good counselling and psychotherapy start with rapport. The therapist must know how to listen and see the world from his client's point of view, while at the same time employing his own skills and qualities. 'Listening' means not only taking in the words, but also the gestures, voice and facial expressions of the client, and even what he leaves unsaid.

By commenting on what is coming across, the therapist helps his client to face his scars and distortions, thus robbing them of their enormous power.

Counselling usually means listening and talking on both sides, but current psychotherapy, particularly in America, uses many techniques – bodywork, meditation, 'acting out' and a range of others – which focus on emotional release and spontaneity and take a very positive approach. They are based on an intense faith in a person's capacity for development and seek not only to free him from the bondage of neurosis, but to enhance his energy, creativity and capacity for joy.

If you think that counselling or psychotherapy might help you, it might be valuable to explain what a therapist is *not*.

He or she is not your parent. The resolution of your conflicts cannot be doled out like sweets; it has to be earned, and you must earn it yourself. A good therapist will co-operate with you and will not try to dominate.

Beware of a therapist who needs you more than you need him, who uses his clients as an excuse to sidestep his own problems and, of course, avoid anyone who does not treat what you tell him as strictly confidential.

Healing and growth can be bumpy. It can be like taking two steps forward and one step back, and, unless you like and trust your therapist, the relationship is not going to work.

Counselling and psychotherapy can be vital for addicts, who not only have to come off their drugs, but may have to go through major inner changes to help themselves stay off. With the best intentions and the best therapies to minimize withdrawals, if the person does not change at the same time, he is still in danger of retreating once again to the drug which comforted him and made reality more bearable before.

Therapeutic groups can also be valuable, replacing a circle of drug-using friends with a group of people who share the experience of coming off. Leaving addiction behind can mean, as well as a radical break with the past, a strain on your own resources at a time when you may feel alone and vulnerable. A group offers you the support you need, and could play an essential part in your permanent recovery.

Please turn to the directory for information on where to find a qualified counsellor or psychotherapist.

Cranial osteopathy

This technique influences the whole body. The practitioner uses a very subtle, hardly detectable touch, usually on the head and sometimes on the pelvis.

In the early 1900s the American osteopath William Garner Sutherland came to disagree with the idea, drawn from anatomists studying corpses, that the skull is rigid. He observed that the edges of certain skull bones were bevelled, notched and angled where they joined or overlapped each other, and concluded that they were, in fact, slightly mobile.

A skilled cranial osteopath can detect a slight expansion and contraction, caused by fluctuations of cerebro-spinal fluid and influencing the brain, the skull bones, the spinal column and the sacrum. This continuous cycle, the 'primary respiratory mechanism', is detectable most easily in the head and pelvis, but it affects the physiology of the whole body.

However, this mechanism is in turn affected by age, general health, emotional stability and any head injury, especially those sustained at birth. By treating it, cranial osteopathy treats the health of the whole person.

A very gentle treatment, it 'is not so much concerned with altering the position of bones as with releasing articular strains between the structures and restoring physiological motion' (*Osteopathy*, Leon Chaitow, Thorsons, 1982). Rough handling is never involved; the patient is aware only of a light, sensitive touch. He usually feels very relaxed and may sometimes even fall asleep. Afterwards, some people feel light-headed for a few moments.

An osteopath trained in this technique may use it on its own or with ordinary osteopathy.

Please turn to the directory for information on where to find a qualified cranial osteopath.

Healing

Healing has always been with us. For early man, it was part of his religion and healer priests were much revered. At the time of the Pharaohs the court favourite, Imhotep (about 2635 to 2570 BC) was famous for his healing powers. He was later believed to inhabit the body of a snake, the symbol of healing ever since. By the third century BC worship of the equally renowned Greek healer, Askepois, had spread to Rome, where his name changed to Aesculapius.

Jesus was the greatest healer priest. He understood that illness could be caused by guilt and often had to forgive people before they would recover. He hoped that his healing would be passed on, and St Luke writes (9: 1 and 2):

> *Then he called his 12 disciples together, and gave them power and authority over all devils, and to cure diseases. And he sent them to preach the kingdom of God, and to heal the sick.*

The early Church continued His work. But later, when purely secular ways of treating the sick had started to spread from Greece, the Church retreated from her healing role, asking her priests for scholastic attainments rather than spiritual gifts.

Now, after centuries of neglect, healing is coming back into the Christian Church. But much healing is done in the West by lay healers; people who, although they may believe that they are channels for spiritual power, are not necessarily enthusiastic church-goers.

Two UK reports, published in 1914 and 1958 – whose members were drawn mostly from the Church and the medical profession – found against healing. In spite of this, however, healing outside the Church has gained momentum in recent years, part of the current interest in holistic, drugless ways of treating illness. In 1965 the National Federation of Spiritual Healers (open to all denominations) was given permission, in spite of furious objections from the British Medical Association, to send their accredited healers into the wards of more than 1,500 hospitals.

Now, there are over 20,000 healers working in the UK, including prayer healers, healing circles in churches, part-time and full-time healers; over 20 doctors use healing.

Most agree that they are channelling some form of energy. This energy works holistically on the mind, spirit and body, and it can have a profound effect on both the patient's attitudes and the quality of his life. But it is not fully understood and healers do not agree about how it actually works.

Although the phenomenon of healing has been proved in the laboratory, analysis is not helpful. But Bruce MacManaway in his book *Healing* (Thorsons, 1983), writes:

> *The vital point is that health is restored, and the fact that we do not fully understand what triggers off the individual's own healing processes is bad for our intellectual egos but of secondary importance.*

Healers come from all walks of life. Many say that almost everyone has the healing gift to some extent or another, and they claim that compassion and love are their driving forces. The late Maxwell Cade, physicist and researcher, had a high opinion of healers. He wrote that most of them had an ability to be open to life, to be calm and still and to release their personal egos, so that they could be in touch with a greater whole.

Some healers diagnose intuitively, some ask their patients directly what is wrong and some use dowsing. Some need to be in the right state of mind to accomplish healing, and others can be absent-minded about it. Healing can work regardless of religious belief, and the patient doesn't have to believe that it is going to help. But the healer needs to have faith in the healing energy, wherever he or she may think it comes from.

Please turn to the directory for information on where to find a healer.

Herbal medicine

Medicinal herbs – camomile, burdock root, dandelion, and many thousands of others – form part of a tradition stretching further back than the earliest man, for we are not the only animals to use plants in this way. A cat, for instance, will often chew grasses when it is ill. Over the centuries, primitive man built on his first, instinctive knowledge and passed it down by word of mouth.

Written guides to herbalism date from about 2200 BC. The father of medicine, Hippocrates (from about 470 to 380 BC) studied and used herbs. Every Roman quartermaster carried garlic for his men, and when Christianity arrived in early Britain the monks gave herbal medicines to the people. The 16th century medical genius, Paracelsus, is often called the patron saint of the drug companies, but he had a profound and wide knowledge of herbal medicine.

In the time of Henry VIII, continuous efforts by the physicians and apothecaries to ban herbalists were frustrated by the Quacks' Charter of 1512. Probably the king himself had used his influence to support the herbalists; his sex life was so active that he needed herbal ointments 'to coole and comfort the Member'. The 17th century English herbalist, Nicholas Culpeper, gave cheap, effective treatment to the poor at his surgery in Spitalfields, and attacked the doctors, saying that because of their greed 'the poor creature for whom Christ died must forfeit his life for want of money.' His *Herbal* has gone through dozens of editions and is still being sold.

Today, courses for professional medical herbalists are bursting at the seams and scientists are finally taking herbal medicine seriously.

During the 1850s, pharmacists were first able to isolate the 'active principle' – that part of a plant responsible for its therapeutic action. They started using the active principle on its own, and were later able to synthesize it. Thus, Peruvian bark gave quinine, deadly nightshade atropine, and the willow tree a forerunner of aspirin.

These new drugs formed part of the plethora of chemicals which orthodox medicine is encouraged to prescribe today.

Herbalists, however, believe that the effect of the active principle is modified and made less harmful by the hundreds of other substances originally accompanying it. So they use only extracts from, or part of, the whole plant. This is the most important difference between herbal medicine and modern drugs.

For example the herb, Rauwolfia, has been used in India for centuries as a sedative and to lower high blood pressure. The plant's active principle is a powerful alkaloid, reserpine. But the drug reserpine (Serpasil) carries with it dangerous side-effects, such as depression, diarrhoea, vertigo and lethargy. These side-effects do not occur if the complete herb is given. Similarly, dandelion is a diuretic; it makes your kidneys work hard. So do some modern drugs, but they cause the body to lose minerals, too, notably potassium. Dandelion has a high potassium content.

Herbal remedies come in several forms. Decoctions and infusions are made by boiling the herb in water, and tinctures by steeping the crushed herb in alcohol and straining the liquid. Juices and poultices are made from fresh herbs. Herbal oils (not the same as essential oils) are made by steeping bruised herbs in vegetable oil.

A herbal prescription is made up for the individual patient, and may contain up to 30 different herbs. The practitioner will also ask about your diet and lifestyle. Treatment takes time.

Medical herbalism is particularly effective with chronic degenerative illnesses – asthma and hay fever, rheumatism and arthritis, digestive, liver and heart conditions – the menopause and PMT, anxiety, depression and tension. It can also be used for chronic infections and skin problems and plays a useful role in addiction to drugs.

Herbal treatment may include the Bach flower remedies, developed by the late Dr Edward Bach, which can be valuable for the emotional and psychological problems often lying at the root of addiction.

Current research into medicinal herbs includes projects set up by the World Health Organization, which is encouraging the use of herbs in the Third World. In an African project, WHO researchers found herbal medicines effective against diabetes, herpes zoster and bronchial asthma.[1] Brazilian scientists are testing native herbs and trying to collect data on them before the destruction of their countryside wipes out the plants as well.[2] In America, researchers at Harvard University and the National Cancer Institute are combing their way through thousands of herbs. British research at Chelsea College and St Bartholomew's Hospital is hampered, however, by lack of funds.

Please turn to the directory for information on where to find a qualified practitioner.

References

1 *World Health* (a WHO publication), November 1977.
2 *Register* (Orange County, California), November 11, 1983.

Homoeopathy

The homoeopathic practitioner believes that symptoms are not the actual disease itself, but discernible signs of the body's fight against it. His job is to help the body win its fight by giving small doses of a drug which, in a healthy person, will produce the same symptoms.

This apparently paradoxical idea that 'like is cured by like', is not new. It was understood by Hippocrates. (Vaccination also stimulates body defences without producing the disease itself, and a few modern orthodox drugs work on a similar principle.) But the man who created modern homoeopathy was a German doctor, Samuel Hahnemann (1755 – 1843).

After years of research and struggle, Hahnemann finally became famous in 1812 when he used homoeopathy on 180 of Napoleon's soldiers who had typhoid. Only one man died. Later, in 1854, a cholera epidemic reached London, and the newly-established homoeopathic hospital took in victims. (This hospital, the Royal London Homoeopathic, now stands in Great Ormond Street.) Over half of the 54,000 people who died had received orthodox treatment. But of the 61 people treated homoeopathically, only 10 died.

In spite of royal patronage, and the fact that most homoeopaths are doctors who have taken an additional qualification, resistance from the medical establishment continues. Those wishing to train still find it difficult because there are no government grants towards the cost of the courses, but fortunately this does not stop more and more doctors from studying homoeopathy.

The remedies

Hahnemann found in his research that, not surprisingly, diluting a drug lessened its toxic effects. But he also found that this dilution intensified the drug's power to cure. He therefore called his dilutions 'potencies'. The more a drug is diluted, the higher its potency.

The remedies are taken from plant, animal and mineral sources. Allium Cepa is made from onion, Argentum nitricum from nitrate of silver, and Apia mellifica from the honey bee. For a demical potency of 1X, one part of the 'mother tincture' (the source material) is mixed well with nine parts of the 'base' (water and/or alcohol). The container is then shaken and struck forcefully against a firm surface, which is believed to enhance the curative energy of the remedy, and the contents added to the tablet material. For 2X, one part of this dilution is mixed with nine parts of the base and shaken (succussed) and so on. For the centesimal potencies, one part of the mother tincture is mixed with 99 drops of the base to make 100C. There are now over 2000 proven homoeopathic remedies.

If you consult a homoeopath, you will be given a prescription specifically chosen for you, and probably dietary advice as well. Homoeopathy treats the individual. Knowing that people of different temperaments react to the same substance in different ways, the homoeopath finds out at the first consultation what kind of person you are. What foods do you prefer? Do you worry a lot? Do you like being surrounded by people? The answers that you give, the impression the homoeopath forms of you, will influence his prescription. The drug he may give on this basis is your constitutional remedy.

The way the patient reacts to the illness is also part of the symptom picture. One child with measles will be iritable, thirsty and touchy, and will not want to be moved. He might be given byronia (wild hops). Another may cry a lot and not be thirsty, but demand constant attention. He might need pulsatilla (wild flower). This matching of characteristics and reactions is the essence of homoeopathy.

Because treatment unlocks illness so that the body can deal with it better, symptoms may occasionally change or even get worse for the moment and the remedy may be changed too. But you do not have to go on 'taking the pills' indefinitely. Homoeopathy aims not for the suppression of symptoms, but for a complete cure. When your vital energies have been restored, and you start to feel better, treatment is usually stopped.

Homoeopathic remedies are also on sale to the public. These are general remedies, mostly for acute conditions, and need only to be matched to symptoms; they can be highly successful.

Homoeopathy is valuable for chronic degenerative illnesses and nervous and psychological disorders. It can resolve an allergy problem and help acute conditions – skin troubles, infections, strains and injuries including post-operative shock, migraine, some eye and throat conditions, colds and catarrh. It is useful for childhood illnesses, including teething. In the treatment of addiction, it can be used both to detoxify the body and, in homoeopathic desensitization techniques, to turn off both the person's craving for the substance and his reaction to it.

Research has established that homoeopathy is more effective than a placebo (an inert substance which tastes and looks the same as the medicine) for rheumatoid arthritis.[1] It has been found to prevent 'flu better than an allopathic treatment.[2] It has worked well in animal trials[3] and, in the laboratory, cells from humans and animals,[4] plants[5] and even yeast[6] responded to homoeopathy.

A summary of recent research[7] lists the successful treatment of whooping cough, allergy to house dust and hay fever with homoeopathic medicine. The Royal London Homoeopathic Hospital is currently researching into low potency remedies, and the National Homoeopathic Research Group is studying the effect of homoeopathy on morning sickness, hay fever, and lead and aluminium poisoning.

Please turn to the directory for information on where to find a qualified practitioner.

References

1 R G Gibson et al, *British Journal of Clinical Pharmacology*, ix: 453 459.
2 D H Livingston et al, *Homoeopathy*, November 1970.
3 C E I Day, *The Veterinary Record*, March 3, 1984.
4 V A Moss et al, *British Homoeopathic Journal*, vol 71, No. 2, April 1982.
5 Raynor L Jones and Michael D Jenkins, *British Homoeopathic Journal*, vol 70, No. 3, July 1981.

6 Raynor L Jones and Michael D Jenkins, *British Homoeopathic Journal*, vol 72, No. 3, July 1983.
7 *Midlands Homoeopathy Research Group Communications*, No. 11, February 1984.

Hypnotherapy

Hypnotherapy is the use of hypnosis as a therapeutic tool. Hypnos was the Greek god of sleep, but the hypnotic trance lies on the peaceful threshold of sleep. It is an altered state of mind in which everyday thinking is suspended, and gates to the unconscious mind are opened. It is this access to our deeper self which gives hypnotherapy its value.

Underneath our conscious, wakeful, mind which sorts out impressions, criticizes, and orders our lives, stretches the vast sea of the unconscious. A reservoir of past thoughts, feelings and experiences, it has a tremendous effect on our attitudes and behaviour. It comes to the surface in dreams, meditations, creative activity, and it can be reached directly, and persuaded to change, during the hypnotic state.

Hypnotherapy can suggest more positive ways of reacting to life and if necessary it can uncover and confront old wounds, robbing them of their ability to hurt and distort. Western thinking is usually overbalanced in favour of the rational, linear approach, and hypnotherapy can help to develop the mind's free-ranging, intuitive side.

When the conscious mind is side-stepped, verbal suggestions given by the hypnotherapist are believed to reach the more primitive parts of the brain along a direct route passing through the limbic system – a receiver open to our emotional states. This 'hot line' is probably what gives these suggestions their peculiar impact.

Between 80 per cent and 90 per cent of people can be hypnotized to varying degrees. Children between seven and fourteen are the best subjects, probably because they daydream and play the most. Among adults, well-adjusted sceptics are the best subjects. (People with psychotic illnesses, including schizophrenia, or those with grand mal epilepsy, should not be treated, nor should very young children.) Animals can be put into a trance by gentle stroking and talking; chickens are particularly good subjects, but those at the top of the pecking order are more resistant than their down-trodden colleagues.

Hypnosis is not a passive state where the manipulated subject does not know what is happening and must submit to the hypnotist's commands, however outrageous they are. Films depicting a Svengali swinging a watch and glaring masterfully at a helpless victim, probably female, are entertaining but inaccurate. Stage hypnosis works because the hypnotist first uses tricks on his audience which help him to select suggestible people who want to show off.

Hypnosis has been used in many religions, by priests in ancient Egypt and classical Greece, by Hindu and Persian holy men, and Indian yogis. But the father of modern hypnotism is Franz Anton Mesmer (1734 – 1815).

The son of a poor Austrian farmer, Mesmer was a brilliant student who finally qualified as a doctor after studying both theology and law. One of his woman patients was very ill with fainting fits, delirium and vomiting, and he treated her successfully by touching her with bars of magnetized iron. From this beginning he evolved the theory that healing was brought about by a natural power which he called animal magnetism. As part of his treatment, he would put his patients into a trance state. Mesmer became the rage of Paris and people would crowd into his large, lavishly furnished consulting room where they would sit round a huge vat filled with water, powdered glass and iron filings, holding the iron bars protruding from it. Mesmer would make his entrance to soft music, dressed in a long robe of lilac silk and carrying an iron rod. As he walked round, he would induce a trance state in his patients, and those who were more excitable would fall at his feet in convulsions. His very theatrical approach worked with many incurable patients, but it outraged the doctors and in 1784 he was discredited. The doctors concluded that, although his cures were manifestly genuine, they could not be explained and so they could not have happened.

Among many fascinated by hypnosis – soon to shed Mesmer's theatricalism – was Sigmund Freud, who at first believed it should be an essential part of psycho-analysis. However, he later became disenchanted with what he saw as a process where the patient himself does not actively get through to his own repressed material. He did not enjoy being stared at by his patients, either, and his distaste deepened when a woman patient, clearly transferring her affections, flung her arms around his neck.

John Elliotson, a brilliant doctor, took up the technique in the 1800s and taught it to the novelist Charles Dickens who used it with disastrous results; the episode nearly wrecked his marriage. Elliotson used hypnotism to replace surgical anaesthesia on many patients, and wrote about the hypnotic treatment of breast cancer.

> *The cancerous mass is now completely dissipated, not the slightest lump is to be found nor is there the slightest tenderness of the bosom or the armpit.*[1]

However, like his contemporaries Esdaile and Braid, he could not get other doctors to accept or even take an interest in his results. By this time, hypnotism had been pared down to essentials – the voice of the therapist getting through to the fixed attention of the patient – and the hypnotic state was charmingly, although fleetingly, dubbed by the Abbé di Paria 'lucid sleep'.

During the First World War, hypnotism proved useful for war neuroses. Its status as a therapy was further confirmed both by the Hypnotism Act of 1952 which limited stage use, and a subsequent BMA report admitting its value.

Hypnotherapists working today make use of two possible approaches – a focusing on symptoms or an exploration of their origins. The former approach is the way hypnotism is traditionally used in the relief of pain – post-operatively and during dentistry and childbirth. Research proved its analgesic effectiveness as long ago as 1932.[2] This direct, non-analytical approach can also be used to reduce tension, anxiety and lack of confidence. The hypnotherapist can encourage his patient's positive, assertive side to grow and become stronger. And by the use of self-hypnosis, a simple technique which the patient uses on his own whenever he needs it, he can learn to cope with many problems independently of the therapist.

In the treatment of habits and addictions this symptomatic treatment is positive, pointing out, for example, how much better a person will feel when he stops smoking. Using aversion therapy – telling him that when he smokes the cigarette will taste of old socks – is less popular now.

However, this does not always go far enough, and some habits serve a purpose – a woman stopped biting her nails, but started pulling her hair out instead. Some conflicts having a profoundly damaging effect on us are not accessible in this way and need an analytical approach. The sources of these conflicts in the unconscious can then be reached and their resolution is a potent force for healing and change. Using hypno-analysis to get to the root of the problem means that the patient can confront the buried part of himself which is causing pain. This foray into the hidden, vulnerable parts of a person needs skilled and sympathetic handling.

We still have a lot to learn about what can be done with hypnosis. Milton Erickson, a charismatic therapist working in the 1940s, saw it not only as a means of resolving mental and physical illness but as a way of galvanizing latent creativity and energy. In *Harpers and Queen*, September 1985, Leslie Kenton wrote:

> *Erickson opened the eyes of psychology to the possibility that hypnosis could be used as a bridge to areas of consciousness embedded deep within human experience on which we could call not only for healing but also for the solving of mathematical problems, the creation of art, the establishment of communication on very deep levels with other human beings.*

Please turn to the directory for information on where to find a qualified practitioner.

References

1 *Hypnosis*, David Waxman (Allen and Unwin, 1981).
2 *Journal of Experimental Psychology* No. 15, 1932.

Nutrition

Hippocrates, the father of medicine, said, 'Let food be your medicine and medicine your food.' He thus anticipated by several centuries one of our fastest-growing areas of modern research – nutritional therapy.

However, the detailed study of vitamins, minerals, fats, fibre and amino acids has been part of scientific advance during only the past few decades. As recently as the early 20th century, food was simply measured in terms of calories and protein.

Vitamins are essential for life. They are made by plants, and some animals, including ourselves, make a few of their own as well. The story of vitamin C is typical – a slow progress towards our current understanding. In the 17th century, when long sea voyages were common, sailors died terrible deaths from the vitamin C deficiency disease, scurvy. Although the herb to cure it, scurvy grass, was already known, it was surgeon's mate James Lind who in 1747 saved a group of sailors from this fatal disease by giving them another, new, treatment – citrus fruits. After this discovery, it was still many years before fresh citrus fruits were stowed in the holds of ships (thus earning the British sailor his nickname of Limey), during which time sailors were dying painful and unnecessary deaths.

Nobody realized that the active part of the fruit which cured scurvy was vitamin C; it was not until 1928 that Albert Szent-Gyorgyi finally isolated it. It is now produced synthetically in several forms, and its use in almost all body processes is being charted. Dr Linus Pauling, winner of two Nobel prizes, has studied vitamin C for years and is examining its effects on cancer.

Minerals are found in the soil, whence they are taken up by

plants. Iron is an essential mineral which many of us lack. Another important mineral, potassium, is needed for energy and heart action, and excess salt deprives the body of potassium – an example of the way all nutrients influence each other.

Although it can be very valuable to use isolated nutrients to treat illness, they do not work alone, but as part of a complex web. Calcium, for example, should be taken with magnesium; zinc and vitamin A need each other to work effectively, and iron needs vitamin C for better absorption.

But what, exactly, *do* we eat?

Our food is changed now during production more than it ever has been. And it is changed, not for our nutritional benefit, but to stop it going bad and to make it sell. Starting with the soil, artificial fertilizers can crowd out and prevent the uptake of natural minerals. If a plant cannot get a balanced spectrum of minerals from the soil, it cannot create them. Animals and humans eating the plant will be deficient too.

Nitrates are found in our soils and waters in increasing and unsafe amounts. When these chemicals reach the stomach, they can change into carcinogens.

Pesticides can cause reactions in sensitive people and there are doubts about their safety. *The Lancet*[2] reported a possible link between pesticides and Parkinson's Disease. Checks carried out in 1983 by the Association of Public Analysts found that *one third* of the fruit and vegetables examined contained significant levels of pesticide residues, including aflatoxin, a powerful carcinogen found in nuts.

Farm livestock is treated with antibiotics, tranquillizers and growth-promoters; existing regulations cannot effectively control the use of these chemicals, and residues may often be left in the carcases.

The food industry is currently bedevilled by public worries about additives. (A recent analysis of an iced bun showed that it contained nine additives, at least four of which can have adverse effects.) Some additives are listed on food labels, but you need to know what these mysterious numbers mean and what the chemicals may do to you. Please see Maurice Hanssen's *The New E for Additives* (Thorsons, 1987)

People are becoming aware, too, of nutritional losses to their food during processing. They are asking not only, 'What chemicals are being put in?' but also, 'What is being processed out?'

Nutrient loss depends on how the food is processed. Vegetables blanched before being canned, frozen or dried can lose up to half their vitamin C (in spite of the fact that frozen vegetables may contain more vitamin C to start with than they would have done wilting at the greengrocer's). Frozen peas and beans washed in EDTA suffer mineral loss. Heating foods to can them destroys B vitamins as well as C, and minerals leach out into the canning liquid, which is usually poured away.

The refining of flour to 70 per cent extraction (wholemeal flour of 100 per cent extraction has all the original germ and bran) involves the loss of between 50 and 100 per cent of over 13 nutrients, and by milling the natural fibre out of our flour, we lose a food element whose deficiency has been linked with many chronic degenerative diseases.

Perhaps, in view of the thousands of chemicals being added to our environment – some of which are harmful – and getting into us, it is not surprising that we are living through a current epidemic of allergic illnesses. Too many of us are allergic to, or intolerant of, common foods. The commonest allergens are milk and wheat, and heavily refined and processed foods cause more trouble than the more natural varieties.

However, in response to public concern, big changes are on the way. Health food stores are crowded. Books about nutrition fill the shelves, and the media discuss healthy eating, sometimes confusingly. People are eating more fruit, salads and vegetables; low fat yoghurts, wholegrain, low-sugar cereals and additive-free foods are appearing in supermarkets. At the end of a shopping day, the bread still unsold is usually white. We are realizing that we do not need vast quantities of fats, sugar and salt, and our consumption of these is dropping.

Most alternative practitioners are aware of the importance of nutrition and, for medical herbalists, naturopaths, and many osteopaths and traditional acupuncturists, it forms part of their training.

The treatment of illness with whole, raw foods has been used by physicians from Hippocrates to the 20th century Dr Bircher-Benner and the cancer genius, Max Gerson, and it is the cornerstone of naturopathy, or nature cure. Virtually ignored by recent medical training, and eclipsed by the plethora of modern drugs enthusiastically promoted by the drug companies, nutrition is coming back into favour among doctors. At the first meeting of the British Society for Nutritional Medicine in

September 1984, more than 80 doctors were present.

Our problem in the West is not starvation. It is the distortion of our food by robbing it of nutrients and treating it with suspect additives. However, these dangers are at last starting to get the attention they deserve both from the medical profession and their patients, the public.

Please turn to the directory for information on where to find a qualified practitioner.

References

1 *British Nutrition Foundation Bulletin* No. 39
2 *Journal of Alternative and Complementary Medicine*, July 1987

Osteopathy

Basically, osteopathy is the treatment of abnormalities in the skeleton and muscles by techniques of adjustment.

The founder of modern osteopathy is Andrew Taylor Still (1828 – 1917). Born in Jonesburgh, Virginia, USA, Still suffered frequent painful headaches as a child. One day, he rested his throbbing head on a swing in the garden so that it was supported just below the base of the skull, and in a few minutes his headache disappeared. Later on in life, he remembered this episode when he began to study the link between skeletal condition and health.

Andrew Still learned medicine from his father and other practising doctors, as there were at that time few medical schools in the US. Later, he attended a medical school in Kansas City and served as a surgeon in the Civil War.

In 1846, his three children died in a meningitis outbreak on the Missouri frontier. He wrote:

Not until my heart had been torn and lacerated with grief and affliction could I fully realize the inefficacy of drugs. Some may say that I should suffer in order that good might come, but I feel that my grief came through gross ignorance on the part of the medical profession.

Still's interest in engineering led him to study the interdependence of structure and function in the human body. He came to the conclusion that, because mechanical disturbance could cause illness elsewhere in the body, some illnesses could be cured by mechanical correction. So he continued to develop the art of manipulation, finding that in many cases it made surgery and drugs unnecessary.

In 1892 the first College of Osteopathy was founded under his auspices in Kirksville and, when he died in 1917, there were over 5,000 osteopathic physicians practising in the US. Although there are today twelve American schools of osteopathy, giving seven years of training, their curricula include a full orthodox medical education as well, so osteopathic physicians in the US tend to be indistinguishable from their colleagues who use drugs and other allopathic treatments.

Osteopathy was first brought to the UK from America in the early 1900s; the British School of Osteopathy was founded in 1918 and it still trains practitioners today.

Osteopathy is one of the most respectable alternative or complementary therapies. Many doctors refer patients for osteopathy, and some think it should be available under the NHS. However, unity still eludes the profession.

Some practitioners use only osteopathy, some include naturopathy as well, and some are doctors who have taken an additional osteopathic qualification.

Theory and practice

Osteopaths believe that the body is always striving to heal itself and will do so, given the chance. The body is vulnerable to disorders of the musculo-skeletal system – bones, ligaments, muscles, fascia – and any disorder of this system can disturb the health of other body parts. Recovery is hampered if this disorder is not corrected.

The musculo-skeletal system's influence is mainly through the nervous system which permeates the whole body and whose function depends partly on the unimpeded flow of nerve impulses and blood. A recent discovery of the fact that nerves carry not only messages but proteins, fats and other cell substances,[1] further emphasizes the importance of the musculo-skeletal system, with its effect on total body health.

An osteopath, therefore, does not simply treat your aching back. He uses manipulation to detect and correct both faulty structure and faulty function throughout the whole body. As well as using a wide range of manipulative techniques, many osteopaths prescribe exercises to correct bad habits and strengthen muscles so that they can easily support better posture and movement. Some will include advice on diet, relaxation, and so on. They may use orthodox methods of diagnosis, including cardiological and laboratory tests and X-rays.

Osteopathy is especially valuable for back ailments, including a 'slipped disc'. (The disc itself does not slip; it herniates so that the inner pulp protrudes, causing spasm in the surrounding muscles and painful pressure on the nerves.)

There are, however, many other conditions which can be successfully treated by osteopathy:

- Allergies – the adrenal glands and the liver are usually affected and both are influenced by spinal disorders
- Arthritis – degeneration cannot be undone, but mobility can be improved
- Asthma – rib mobility, which is often restricted, can be improved
- Bronchitis – breathing and mucus elimination can be made easier
- Constipation – can be cured (using diet as well)
- Digestive complaints – can be helped when the spine is involved
- Headaches – some can be cured
- Heart problems – an upper chest lesion may be misdiagnosed as angina. In genuine heart conditions, discomfort can be reduced
- Hiatus hernia – symptoms can be minimized
- Hypertension – if the result of tension, it can be reduced
- Menstrual problems – trouble often originates in incorrect angulation of the lower spine, and this can be treated
- Sciatica – can sometimes be helped
- Stress and tension – can often be reduced.

Please turn to the directory for information on where to find a qualified practitioner.

Reference

1 *Osteopathy*, Leon Chaitow (Thorsons, 1982).

Transcendental Meditation

Meditation in various forms has been practised from the days of our primitive ancestors. Later, meditators used words or sounds – mantras – to calm the mind and increase its power. Although we associate meditation with stillness and solitude, some forms call for ritualized movement. But, whether used by a Tibetan monk or an executive with his feet up in the lunch hour, meditation is an altered state of consciousness.

In India and many parts of Asia meditation has been refined and developed since the dawn of recorded history, and it forms part of yoga. In the West, it became a part of religious observance. No longer principally used to clear the mind of its ceaseless chattering, it helped the votary to communicate with God.

Now, Western meditators use several forms. Visualization – seeing a tumour dissolve with the mind's eye, or immune cells multiplying – is helping cancer patients to recover, and is incorporated in alternative treatments for AIDS. The Silva method of mind control uses active imagination to enhance people's effectiveness and the quality of their lives. Meditation is practised by the growing number of Western Buddhists, and it is included in the later stages of Autogenics, or AT, a relaxation system designed by German neurologist Schultz.

The best-known kind of meditation used now in the West is Transcendental Meditation (TM). It was developed by the Maharishi Mahesh Yogi, a physics and chemistry graduate who studied for many years under another Indian mystic and sage, Guru Dev. After his master's death, Maharishi spent two years of solitude in a Himalayan cave before deciding to go out into the world where, for the past 20 years, he has been teaching and spreading knowledge about TM.

He has founded the International Meditation Society, the Maharishi International University, and the Foundation for the Science of Creative Intelligence. During the Sixties, TM became a cult, taken up by the hippies and by the Beatles. It is now taught in almost every country in the world.

The Maharishi, like many other thinkers, sees the world at crisis point. We are being overwhelmed by intellectually derived technology, with its attendant pollution and rapid change, but we lack the emotional and spiritual maturity to deal with it. He believes that TM, with its development of these qualities in man, is one important way to avoid the global catastrophe which threatens us.

Used in this way, meditation should be *effortless*. It does not involve striving to focus or discipline a rebellious and over-active mind. The meditator, who learns the technique from a trained instructor, uses it for about 20 minutes twice a day. He or she mentally repeats a specially chosen mantra, which has no significance and which therefore does not start any train of thought.

Effects

On the physical level TM (in common with relaxation techniques) offers effective, profound relief from stress. It shares with AT and several other systems the ability to reduce high blood pressure[1] and slows down both heart[2] and breathing rates[3] in an unforced way. Skin conductivity, which goes up with stress, is also lowered,[4] as is blood lactate[5] (produced during strenuous exercise and associated with feelings of anxiety), together with blood levels of a stress hormone, cortisol.[6]

In addition, TM tends to balance up brain function between the two hemispheres. The left hemisphere is the major controller of language and rational functions – linear thinking – and the right hemisphere is largely responsible for spatial relationships, image recognition and aesthetic appreciation – simultaneous, parallel thinking. In our culture, right-hemisphere dominance is encouraged at the expense of the less tangible, more intuitive, left-side activity. But meditation goes much further than this and, to fully explain its effects, Maharishi has explored the nature of thought itself.

We do not see a bubble when it starts its rise from the bottom of the pond; we only see it when it breaks the surface. In the same way, we only become conscious of a thought when it breaks into our awareness, but it has risen from the depths of the mind. Maharishi believes that if we could trace a mental experience back to where it was on the point of being generated, we would reach a state of 'zero activity, a state of non-vibrating consciousness'[7] – mental stillness itself.

Each thought is a change of some kind, and he sees all change as natural creative energy at work. The meaning of the thought he sees as the expression of intelligence which gives direction and order to the change. The bedrock source of thought, therefore, is a field of pure creative intelligence.

During meditation, the chatter and fidget of the mind are stilled. The meditator becomes conscious of the subtler, lower stream of thought – the still, small voice – and eventually the mind comes to rest on the field of creative intelligence itself. This peaceful state of inner silence is deeply satisfying and helps him or her to develop intuitive powers and to allow inner healing and growth. He grows into a greater awareness of his relationship to, and dependence upon, the natural world around him – people, animals, plants, the whole planet.

A higher state of consciousness is in essence an inner change, but with this inner change come many changes in one's outer life.[7]

Maharishi feels that if only small numbers of people meditate in each country, this enhances the quality of life for everyone, and he quotes – rather sweepingly perhaps – contrasting crime statistics in various cities which he believes support this idea.

Researchers have found that people who meditate reduce their consumption of various drugs without vast efforts. Narcotics (including heroin),[6] alcohol[8] and tobacco use[9] can all be cut down by meditation.

Please turn to the directory for information on where to learn TM.

References

1 H Benson and R K Wallace, *Circulation*, 45 and 46. Supplement 11.
2 R Keith Wallace, *Science*, 167.
3 K Wallace and H Benson, *Scientific American*, 226: 2.
4 Wallace, Benson and Wilson, *Pychosomatic Medicine*, 35: 4.

5 H Benson and R K Wallace, *American Journal of Physiology*, 221: 3.
6 A Aron and E N Aron, *Addictive Behaviours*, 5 (1980).
7 *The TM Technique*, Peter Russell (Routledge & Kegan Paul, 1977).
8 M Shafh et al, *American Journal of Psychiatry*, 132 (1975).
9 M Shafh et al: *MERU Journal*, 24: 29 (1976).

Part Three
Directory

Section One:
Organizations and
professional associations

You can write to the professional associations listed here for a list of their qualified practitioners; please enclose a 9″ × 6″ stamped and addressed envelope.

For your nearest practitioner, it may be easier to telephone.

Acupuncture

Here are the main organizations:

The British Acupuncture Association and Register Limited,
34 Alderney Street, London SW1V 4EU
Telephone: 01 834 1012

The Traditional Acupuncture Society,
11 Grange Park, Stratford upon Avon CV37 6XH
Telephone: 0789 298798

International College of Oriental Medicine (UK) Limited,
Green Hedges House, Green Hedges Avenue,
East Grinstead, Sussex RH19 1DZ
Telephone: 0342 28567

British Medical Acupuncture Society,
67 Chancery Lane, London WC2 1AF
No telephone enquiries. Membership of doctors only.

Council for Acupuncture,
11 Albany Road, Stratford upon Avon CV27 6PG
Will supply a register including all acupuncturists except doctors for £1.50

Alcohol

Here is a list of organizations who help with alcohol addiction:

ACCEPT (Addictions Community Centres for Education,
Prevention, Treatment)
Activities: art, exercise, relaxation; drugs prescribed.
Nationwide HQ: 200 Seagrave Road, London SW6 1RQ
Tel: 01 381 3155

Al-Anon family groups
Help for families and friends of problem drinkers.
Nationwide HQ: 61 Great Dover Street, London SE1 4YF
Tel: 01 403 0888

Alcohol Concern
For information on national network of local centres contact:
305 Gray's Inn Road, London WC1X 8QF
Tel: 01 833 3471

Alcoholics Anonymous (AA)
Meetings to help problem drinkers. Contact the following
addresses or look in your local telephone directory.
Nationwide HQ: PO Box 1, Stonebow House, Stonebow, York
YO1 2NJ
Tel: 0904 644026/7/8/9

London: 11 Redcliffe Gardens, London SW10
Tel: 01 352 9779
Belfast: 153 Lisburn Road, Belfast, BT9 6AJ Tel: 0232 681084
Wales: Tel: 0222 373939

Drinkwatchers
For those who simply want to cut down.
Nationwide HQ: 200 Seagrave Road, London SW6 1RQ
Tel: 01 381 3157

Medical Council On Alcoholism
Background information:
1 St Andrew's Place, Regent's Park, London NW1 4LB
Tel: 01 487 4445

London only
Greater London Alcohol Advisory Service

Gives the nearest group and borough services in London.
91 Charterhouse Street, London EC1M 6HR
Tel: 01 253 6221

Caffeine

Please see *Nutrition*

Cocaine

Please see *Drugs in general*

Concessions register

A nationwide list of concessions available for complementary
treatment. For information about alternative practitioners
willing to treat patients for a reduced fee, please write to David
Burke at: 36 Broadway Market, Hackney, London E8 4QJ
Telephone: 01 254 1158

Counselling and psychotherapy

The line between counselling and psychotherapy is blurred, but
in general the qualified psychotherapist has taken a longer and
more detailed training than the qualified counsellor. Skilled
counselling, however, is often all that a person needs.

The British Association for Counselling. For information on
individual counsellors and counselling agencies nationwide:
37a Sheep Street, Rugby, Warwickshire CV21 3BX
Tel: 0788 78328/9
They also publish the *Counselling Resources Directory*. Ask your
local library for a copy.

The British Association of Psychotherapists trains its own
practitioners and will give information on other qualifications
too. It is at:
121 Hendon Lane, London N3 3PR
Tel: 01 346 1747

NAYPCAS (National Association of Young People's
Counselling and Advisory Service) Information on counselling
and advisory services for young people nationwide. Letter
service only:

17-23 Albion Street, Leicester, LE1 6GD

The Samaritans,
Telephone counselling service.
HQ: 17 Uxbridge Road, Slough, Berkshire SL1 1SN
Branches throughout the country are listed in the telephone
directories.

Cranial osteopathy

The Cranial Osteopathic Association,
478 Baker Street, Enfield, Middlesex, EN1 3QS
Tel: 01 367 5561
or:
The General Council and Register of Osteopaths (see
Osteopathy). No distinction is made on the Register for those
trained in cranial work. However, the Council can recommend
practitioners.

Drugs in general

ACCEPT (see *Alcohol*, but ACCEPT also offers services on
other drugs)

Families Anonymous,
88 Caledonian Road, London N1
Tel: 01 278 8805 (24 hours)
Nationwide groups for families and friends of drug users.

Institute for the Study of Drug Dependence,
1-4 Hatton Place, Hatton Garden, London EC1N 8ND
Tel: 01 430 1991
Up-to-date material on drug misuse. Comprehensive library.

Narcotics Anonymous (NA)
Tel: 01 351 6794/6066 (24 hours)
Nationwide groups for drug users.
Also: Bristol: PO Box 285, Bristol BS99 7AS Tel: 0272 40084
      Ireland: PO Box 1368, Sherriff Street, Dublin 1, Eire.
      Tel: 0001 300944 ext. 486.

Release,
169 Commercial Street, London E1 3BW
Tel: 01 603 8654 (24 hours) and 01 377 5905
Advice information and referral on drug-related problems
(including legal).

SCODA (Standing Conference on Drug Abuse)
1-4 Hatton Place, Hatton Garden, London EC1N 8ND
Tel: 01 430 2341/2 or Dial 100 and ask for Freephone Drug Problems
Scotland (Scottish Drugs Forum): Tel 041 221 1175
Wales (All Wales Drugsline): Tel: 0222 383313
Nationwide co-ordination of drug organizations and agencies; publishes *Drug Problems: where to get help*: SCODA *National directory* (BBC Publications, 1986).

Turning point,
Cap House, 9-12 Long Lane, London EC1A 9HA
Tel: 01 606 3947
Dale House, New Meeting Street, Birmingham B4 7SX
Tel: 021 632 6364
This is an agency to put you in touch with rehabilitation centres nationwide.

Healing

(Usually free of charge; donations can be accepted)

Absent healing can be very effective; you do not have to visit the healer or even be directly known to him or her. The following can therefore offer nationwide services:

The National Federation of Spiritual Healers,
Old Manor Farm Studio, Church Street, Sunbury-on-Thames, Middlesex TW16 6RG
Tel: 0932 783164 (24 hours)

The Harry Edwards Spiritual Healing Sanctuary,
Burrows Lea, Shere, Guildford, Surrey GU5 9QG
Tel: 048641 2054 (24 hours)

The White Eagle Lodge,
New Lands, Brewells Lane, Rake, Liss, Hampshire GU33 7HY
Tel: 0730 893300

Finding a healer

The Confederation of Healing Organizations,
113 Hampstead Way, London NW11 7JN
Tel: 01 455 2638 (24 hours)

They will put you in touch with an organization to suit you.

The National Federation of Spiritual Healers
(See above) has a nationwide list of its accredited healers.

The Churches' Council For Health and Healing
Marylebone Parish Church, Marylebone Road, London NW1
Tel: 01 486 9644 (24 hours)
They will give information on many healing organizations within
the Church.

Herbalism

To find a qualified medical herbalist, please contact:
Janet Hicks, MNIMH, Secretary, National Institute of Medical
Herbalists, 41 Hatherley Road, Winchester, Hampshire
SO22 6PR
Tel: 0962 68776

Heroin

Please see *Drugs in general*

Homoeopathy

For a list of doctors who have taken a training in homoeopathy
contact:

The British Homoeopathic Association,
27a Devonshire Street, London W1
Tel: 01 935 2163

For a list of lay homoeopathic practitioners contact:

The Society of Homoeopaths,
2a Bedford Place, Southampton, Hampshire SO1 2BY
Tel: 0703 222364

Hypnotherapy

Here are the most reputable professional associations:

The Association of Professional Therapists,
37b New Cavendish Street, London W1M 8JR
Tel: 01 486 4553

British Hypnotherapy Association,
67 Upper Berkeley Street, London W1H 7DH
Tel: 01 723 4443

British Society of Experimental and Clinical Hypnosis,
PO Box 133, Canterbury CT2 7YS
Tel: 0227 738382 ext. 325

British Society of Medical and Dental Hypnosis,
49 Links Road, Ashtead, Surrey KT21 2HJ
Tel: 03722 73522

The National Council of Psychotherapists and Hypnotherapy
Register,
The Glebe House, Pevensey, East Sussex BH24 5LD

or:

The National Council membership list is available from:
1 Clovelly Road, Ealing, London W5
Tel: 01 567 0262 *or* 01 840 3790

The UK Training Training College of Hypnotherapy and
Counselling,
College House, 10 Alexander Street, London W2 8JR
Tel: 01 221 1796/727 2006

Institute for Complementary Medicine
21 Portland Place, London W1N 3AF
Tel: 01 636 9543
Information on all aspects of alternative and complementary
medicine.

Nicotine

ASH (Action on Smoking and Health),
5-11 Mortimer Street, London W1H 7RH
Tel: 01 637 9843
ASH publish an anti-smoking pack. Please send 20p in stamps
with SAE.

Anti-smoking clinics
Please consult your local health education officer.

Anti-smoking yoga tuition
Dr Robin Monro,

Yoga Biomedical Trust, PO Box 140, Cambridge CB1 1PU
Results claimed to be slow but permanent.

Nutrition

Part of the training of all naturopaths and medical herbalists,
and some acupuncturists and osteopaths.
For a dietary therapist, please contact:
The Dietary Therapy Society,
33 Priory Gardens, London N6 5QU
Tel: 01 341 7260

Osteopathy

The British College of Osteopathy and Naturopathy,
6 Netherall Gardens, London NW3 5RR
Tel: 01 435 7830
(List of graduates also available in some libraries.)

The General Council and Register of Osteopaths,
1-4 Suffolk Street, London SW1Y 4HG
Tel: 01 839 2060

The London College of Osteopathic Medicine (part-time
training for doctors),
8-10 Boston Place, London NW1
Tel: 01 262 5250/1128

Psychotherapy

Please see Counselling and Psychotherapy.

Relaxation

Relaxation For Living
Dunesk, 29 Burwood Park Road, Walton-on-Thames, Surrey
KT12 5LH
Classes and teachers all over the country; tapes, leaflets and a
correspondence course available.

Sugar

Please see *Nutrition*

Transcendental Meditation

For information on nationwide classes and teachers contact:
Transcendental Meditation, Freepost, London SW1P 4YY
Tel: Freephone 0800 269303

Tranquillizers

MIND (National Association for Mental Health),
22 Harley Street, London W1N 2ED
Tel: 01 637 0741
Co-ordinates nationwide self-help withdrawal groups.

TRANX (National Tranquillizer Advice Centre),
25a Masons Avenue, Wealdstone, Harrow, Middlesex
HA3 5AH
Tel: 01 863 9716/01 427 2827 (24 hours)
       01 427 2065 (limited hours)
Harrow is the main branch, but there are a few affiliated groups
in other parts of the UK.

ACCEPT (see *Alcohol*)
Can advise on coming off tranquillizers as well.

Please also see *Drugs in general*.

Section Two:
Practitioners and clinics

Practitioners and clinics are listed alphabetically, using their addresses. I have withheld names in almost every case; this is because many professional organizations do not wish the names of their members to be published.

Please note that if a patient genuinely cannot afford the fees, reductions are often possible (please also see Concessions Register in the first section of the directory).

England

Avon

Bath Natural Health Clinic
Alexander House, James Street West, Bath.
Tel: 0225 313153

Addictions treated:
Heroin, alcohol, tranquillizers, nicotine, caffeine, sugar.
Therapies used:
Acupuncture, herbal medicine, hypnotherapy, yoga, massage, diet.
Cost:
First consultation: Between £15 and £25.
Subsequent treatments: Between £10 and £15.

The Practitioner
7 Stanley Road West, Oldfield Park, Bath BA2 3HU
Tel: 0225 318916

Addictions treated:
Nicotine, alcohol, tranquillizers, sugar.
Therapies used:
Hypnotherapy, psychotherapy.
Cost:
£15 per session.

Clifton Counselling Clinic
33 Bellevue Crescent, Clifton Wood, Bristol BS8 4TE
Tel: 0272 297730

Addictions treated:
Cocaine, nicotine, alcohol, tranquillizers, caffeine, sugar.
Therapies used:
Counselling and psychotherapy, hypnotherapy, homoeopathy,
nutrition and supplements, healing, allergy testing.
Cost:
£12 to £14 per half-hour.
£20 to £25 per hour.

Natural Health Clinic
39 Cotham Hill, Bristol BS6 6JY
Tel: 0272 741199

Addictions treated:
Nicotine, tranquillizers, sugar, caffeine.
Therapies used:
Acupuncture, medical herbalism, hypnotherapy, desensitization,
nutrition and supplements, relaxation, counselling, NLP
(neuro-linguistic therapy, or vocal expression).
Cost:
Between £7 and £20 per session.

The Practitioner
527 Gloucester Road, Horfield Common, Bristol BS7 8UG
Tel: 0454 773810

Addictions treated:
Nicotine, alcohol, tranquillizers, caffeine, sugar.
Therapy used:
Medical herbalism.
Cost:
First consultation plus medication: £23

Subsequent consultation and medication: £16

The Clinic
Rocklands, 88 Ridgeway Road, Long Ashton, Bristol
BS18 9HA
Tel: 0272 392203 and 393869

Addictions treated:
Cocaine, nicotine, alcohol, tranquillizers, sugar, caffeine.
Therapies used:
Hypnotherapy, psychotherapy and counselling, homoeopathy,
herbal medicine, aromatherapy, relaxation.
Cost:
£20 per session

The Practitioner
23 Hill Road, Weston-super-Mare, Avon.
Tel: 0749 75352 for appointments.

Addictions treated:
Tranquillizers, alcohol, nicotine, sugar, caffeine.
Therapy used:
Medical herbalism.
Cost:
Please enquire.

Bedfordshire

The Natural Healing Clinic
Ark Farm, Edlesborough, Dunstable, Bedfordshire
Tel: 0525 220139

Addictions treated:
Nicotine, alcohol, tranquillizers, sugar, caffeine.
Therapies used:
Homoeopathy, aromatherapy, nutrition and supplements,
reflexology, counselling and healing, acupressure (treatment
related to acupuncture), Bach flower remedies.
Cost:
First consultation £17
Subsequent treatments: £12

Scotby House
37 Great Northern Road, Dunstable, Bedfordshire LU5 4BN
Tel: 0582 68417

Addictions treated:
Nicotine, tranquillizers.
Therapy used:
Acupuncture.
Cost:
Tobacco: 6 treatments for £30
Please enquire about other rates.

Berkshire

Natural Therapy Clinic
3 Risborough Road, Maidenhead, Berkshire SL6 7BJ
Tel: 0628 72005

Addictions treated:
Heroin, nicotine, alcohol, tranquillizers, caffeine, sugar.
Therapies used:
Hypnotherapy, acupuncture, counselling.
Cost:
First consultation £16
Subsequent consultations £14

The Practitioner
Ridgedale, Allison Gardens, Purley-on-Thames, Pangbourne,
Reading RG8 8DF
Tel: 0734 422955

Addictions treated:
Nicotine, tranquillizers, sugar.
Therapies used:
Hypnotherapy, counselling, homoeopathy.
Cost:
£30 per session.

Buckinghamshire

The Practitioner
14 Cumberland Close, Aylesbury, Buckinghamshire
HP21 7HH
Tel: 0296 86911

Addiction treated:
Nicotine.
Therapy used:
Hypnotherapy; occasionally Bach Flower remedies.
Cost:
£15 per session.

The Practitioner
2 Ramworth Way, Aylesbury, Bucks HP21 7EU
Tel: 0296 26742

Addictions treated:
Tranquillizers, sugar.
Therapies used:
Hypnotherapy, psychotherapy, drama therapy.
Cost:
£15 per hour

Habitbreaker
Bovingdon, Marlow Common, Bucks SL7 2QR
Tel: 06284 75983 (Courses run in London)

Addiction treated:
Nicotine.
Therapy used:
A behavioural modification technique.
Cost:
Course: £150 + VAT.

Cheshire

The Practitioner
1 Graysands Road, Hale, Altrincham, Cheshire WA15 8RY
Tel: 061 928 9777

Addictions treated:
Nicotine, tranquillizers, alcohol, sugar.
Therapies used:
Psychotherapy, hypnotherapy.
Cost:
£20 per session.

The Natural Health Clinic

133 Gatley Road, Gatley, Cheadle, Cheshire SK8 2PD
Tel: 061 428 4980

Addictions treated:
Nicotine, tranquillizers, alcohol, sugar, caffeine.
Therapies used:
Nutrition, acupuncture, herbal remedies, supplements, clinical kinesiology (muscle testing techniques).
Cost:
£20 per session.

The Springfield Clinic of Natural Healing
Springfield House, Newgate, Wilmslow, Cheshire SK9 5LL
Tel: 0625 523155

Addictions treated:
Nicotine, alcohol, tranquillizers, caffeine, sugar.
Therapies used:
Psychotherapy, hypnotherapy, relaxation, medical herbalism.
Cost:
£10 per session, plus medication.

Cornwall

The Shalom Charity Trust
Shalom, Haye Mill, Callington, Cornwall.
No telephone number given.

Addictions treated:
Nicotine, tranquillizers, sugar, caffeine.
Therapies used:
Healing, counselling, prayer.
Cost:
Shalom is a charity; costs vary.

The Lister Centre
32 Lister Street, Falmouth, Cornwall TR11 3BS
Tel: 0326 318973

Addictions treated:
Tranquillizers, nicotine, alcohol, caffeine, sugar.
Therapies used:
Hypnotherapy, reflexology.

Cost:
£25 per session.

Penzance Natural Health Centre
53 Morrah Road, Penzance, Cornwall.
Tel: 0736 60522

Addictions treated:
Nicotine, tranquillizers, sugar.
Therapies used:
Homoeopathy, acupuncture, hypnotherapy.
Cost:
Between £10 and £20 per session.

The Wellbeing Centre
Old School House, Churchtown, Illogan, Redruth, Cornwall.
Tel: 0209 842999

Addiction treated:
Nicotine.
Therapy used:
Hypnotherapy.
Cost:
£15 per 45 minute session.

Hunter's Lodge Clinic
Hunter's Lodge, Lanner Moor, Lanner, Redruth, Cornwall
TR16 6HP
Tel: 0209 214693

Addictions treated:
Nicotine, tranquillizers, sugar, caffeine.
Therapies used:
Acupuncture, osteopathy and cranial osteopathy, massage,
biomagnetism, allergy tests, homoeopathy.
Cost:
Between £15 and £20 per session.

St Austell Natural Health Centre
15b Truro Road, St Austell, Cornwall.
Tel: 0326 (Falmouth number) 318973

Addictions treated:
Tranquillizers, nicotine, alcohol, sugar.

Therapy used:
Hypnotherapy.
Cost:
£25 per session.

Truro Natural Health Centre
5 Station Road, Truro, Cornwall.
Tel: 0872 40321

Addictions treated:
Heroin, cocaine, nicotine, alcohol, tranquillizers, caffeine,
sugar.
Therapies used:
Homoeopathy, hypnotherapy, acupuncture, counselling.
Cost:
Between £10 and £20 per hour.

Devon

Rutt House Clinic
Ivybridge, Devon, PL21 0DQ
Tel: 0752 892792

Addictions treated:
Tranquillizers, nicotine, sugar.
Therapies used:
Allergy tests, homoeopathy, de-sensitization, nutritional advice,
supplements.
Cost:
Initial consultation: £25 including remedies.
Subsequent consultations: £15
Allergy testing: £30

Alternative Treatment Centre
Heddon Hall, Parracombe, Devon EX31 4QL
Tel: 05983 332

Addictions treated:
Cocaine, nicotine, alcohol, tranquillizers, sugar, caffeine.
Therapies used:
Homoeopathy, acupuncture, Bach flower remedies, nutrition,
applied kiniesiology (Touch for Health).

Cost:
£17 per session.

Plymouth Natural Health and Healing Centre
100 Lipsom Road, Plymouth, Devon.
No telephone at the clinic.
Chairman: 0752 660712
Vice Chairman: 0752 822304
Secretary: 0752 228785

Addictions treated:
Heroin, cocaine, nicotine, alcohol, tranquillizers, sugar, caffeine.
Therapies used:
Nutrition, relaxation, meditation and healing, reflexology, shiatsu massage, yoga, counselling, acupuncture, homoeopathy.
Cost:
Mostly free; donations accepted.
For acupuncture and homoeopathy: Between £10 and £25 per session.

The Practitioner
13 The Walronds, Tiverton, Devon EX16 5EA
Tel: 0884 253820

Addictions treated:
Heroin, nicotine, alcohol, tranquillizers.
Therapies used:
Psychotherapy, nutrition and supplements.
Cost:
From £5 to £25 per session.

The Practitioner
91 Sherwell Valley Road, Chelston, Torquay, Devon.
Tel: 0803 605434

Addictions treated:
Nicotine, alcohol, tranquillizers.
Therapies used:
Hypnotherapy, counselling, relaxation.
Cost:
£16 per one-hour session.

District Drug Problem Team

Belmont Court, 124 Newton Road, Torquay, Devon.
Tel: 0803 615741

Addictions treated:
Heroin, tranquillizers.
Therapy used:
Electro-acupuncture.
Cost:
Available under the National Health Service: no charge.

The Devon Clinic of Advanced Natural Medicine
Whitwell, Colyford, Colyton, East Devon EX13 6HS
Tel: 0297 52566

Addictions treated:
Tranquillizers, sugar, caffeine.
Therapies used:
Iridology (diagnosis by examination of the eyes), Touch for
Health, allergy tests, homoeopathy. The main approach is
through nutrition.
Cost:
Whole treatment: £29 plus medication.

Dorset

Herbal Clinic
736b Christchurch Road, Boscombe, Bournemouth, Dorset
BH7 6AQ
Tel: 0202 303904

Addictions treated:
Alcohol, tranquillizers, sugar, caffeine.
Therapy used:
Medical herbalism.
Cost:
First consultation: £11 including medicines.
Subsequent consultation: £8 including medicines.

Bournemouth Centre of Complementary Medicine
26 Sea Road, Boscombe, Bournemouth, Dorset BH5 1DF
Tel: 0202 36354

Addictions treated:
Nicotine, tranquillizers.

Therapies used:
Psychotherapy, hypnotherapy, nutrition and supplements, colon
hydrotherapy, other water treatments, hydrogen peroxide,
Schweitzer fluid.
Cost:
Mainly residential, at about £200 a week.

Whiteways
13 Cowper Road, Bournemouth, Dorset BH9 2UJ
Tel: 0202 512382

Addictions treated:
Alcohol, tranquillizers, sugar, caffeine.
Therapies used:
Medical herbalism, nutrition, meditation, counselling, exercise.
Cost:
Please enquire.

The Practitioner
15 Ensbury Avenue, Bournemouth, Dorset BH10 4HF
Tel: 0202 528504

Addiction treated:
Tranquillizers
Therapies used:
Medical herbalism and counselling.
Cost:
First consultation £12 for one hour.
Subsequent consultations: £5 for half an hour.
Medicines: about £1.50 a week.

Wessex Healthy Living Foundation
72 Belle Vue Road, Southbourne, Bournemouth, Dorset
BH6 3DX
Tel: 0202 422087

Addictions treated:
Nicotine, alcohol, tranquillizers, sugar, caffeine.
Therapies used:
Homoeopathy, nutrition, psychotherapy, reflexology, remedial
massage, acupressure.
Cost:
Initial consultation: £3
Subsequent consultations: between £5 and £12

Bridport Alternative Medicine Practice
50 Victoria Grove, Bridport, Dorset DT6 3AD
Tel: 0308 22644

Addiction treated:
Tranquillizers.
Therapy used:
Homoeopathy.
Cost:
First consultation: £25
Subsequent consultations: £17

Christchurch Clinic of Traditional Chinese Acupuncture
7 St Catherine's Parade, Fairmile Road, Christchurch, Dorset
BH23 2LQ
Tel: 0202 470669

Addictions treated:
Cocaine, nicotine, alcohol, tranquillizers, sugar, caffeine.
Therapies used:
Acupuncture, Bach flower remedies.
Cost:
First consultation: £24
Subsequent treatments: £12.50

The Candida and Colon Clinic
93 Cheap Street, Sherborne, Dorset DT9 3LS
Tel: 0935 813257

Addictions treated:
Nicotine, alcohol, tranquillizers, sugar, caffeine.
Therapies used:
Acupressure (a form of acupuncture), iridology (diagnosis by
examination of the eyes), herbal medicine, nutrition, colonic
irrigation, allergy testing and glucose tolerance testing.
Cost:
£25 per session
Colonic irrigation £30
Glucose tolerance test: £50

Durham

The Herbalist
133 Newgate Street, Bishop Auckland, Durham.
Tel: 0388 60833

Addictions treated:
Nicotine, alcohol, tranquillizers, sugar.
Therapies used:
Hypnotherapy, medical herbalism, homoeopathy, aromatherapy.
Cost:
£10 per session.
Remedies about £1.50 each.

Essex

Homoeopathic, Massage and Hypnotherapy Clinic
Brierley, Main Road, Boreham, Chelmsford, Essex CM3 3JF
Tel: 0245 469851

Addictions treated:
Tranquillizers, nicotine, sugar, caffeine.
Therapies used:
Homoeopathy, hypnotherapy, ear acupuncture, naturopathy, nutrition.
Cost:
About £10 per session.

The Practitioner
24 Kingswood Road, Colchester, Essex CO4 5JX
Tel: 0206 851132

Addictions treated:
Nicotine, alcohol, tranquillizers, sugar, caffeine.
Therapies used:
Hypnotherapy, counselling and psychotherapy, Bach flower remedies, essential oils, healing.
Cost:
£15 per session.

The Practitioner
j50 Third Avenue, Frinton-on-Sea, Essex CO13 9EE
Tel: 02556 2031

Addictions treated:
Tranquillizers, alcohol, nicotine, sugar, caffeine.
Therapies used:
Hypnotherapy, psychotherapy, healing.

Cost:
£20 per consultation.

The Practitioners
2a Cross Road, Romford, Essex RM7 8AT
Tel: 0708 764740

Addictions treated:
Nicotine, alcohol, tranquillizers, sugar, caffeine.
Therapies used:
Hypnotherapy and psychotherapy.
Cost:
First consultation of 2 hours: £20
Subsequent sessions: £15

Acupuncture Centre
38a London Road, Romford, Essex.
Tel: 0708 25610

Addictions treated:
Heroin, nicotine, alcohol, sugar, caffeine.
Therapy used:
Acupuncture.
Cost:
£15 per session.

Natural Health Clinic
14 Olive Street, Romford, Essex RM7 7DS
Tel: 0708 22633

Addiction treated:
Tranquillizers.
Therapies used:
Herbal medicine, aromatherapy, nutrition.
Cost:
Between £17 and £25 a treatment.

The Practitioner
Dolphin House, 6 Gold Street, Saffron Walden, Essex
CB10 1EJ
Tel: 0799 26138

Addictions treated:
Heroin, cocaine, nicotine, alcohol, tranquillizers, caffeine,
sugar.
Therapies used:
Iridology (diagnosis by examination of the eyes), herbal
medicine, homoeopathy, naturopathy, nutrition, Bach flower
remedies.
Cost:
First consultation: £20
Subsequent consultations: £15

The Natural Healing Centre
27 Braintree Road, Witham, Essex.
Tel: 0376 511069

Addictions treated:
Heroin, cocaine, nicotine, alcohol, tranquillizers, sugar,
caffeine.
Therapies used:
Acupuncture, medical herbalism, homoeopathy, hypnotherapy,
yoga, meditation.
Cost:
£12 to £15 per session.

The Practitioner
95 Prospect Road, Woodford Green, Essex.
Tel: 01 505 8720

Addiction treated:
Nicotine.
Therapy used:
Hypnotherapy.
Cost:
Please enquire.

Gloucestershire

The Cheltenham Holistic Health Centre
9 Imperial Square, Cheltenham.
Tel: 0242 584140

Addictions treated:
Heroin, nicotine, alcohol, tranquillizers, caffeine, sugar.

Therapies used:
Acupuncture, aromatherapy, remedial massage, herbal medicine.
Cost:
Between £11 and £20 per consultation.
Medicines: £2 per week.

Edward Waite Healing Centre
41 Ruspidge Road, Cinderford, Gloucestershire GL14 3AE
Tel: 0594 24944

Addictions treated:
Heroin, cocaine, nicotine, alcohol, tranquillizers, sugar, caffeine.
Therapy used:
Contact and absent healing.
Cost:
Contact healing: £5 per session.
Absent healing: free of charge.

Cirencester Natural Therapies
14 Dollar Street, Cirencester.
Tel: 0285 66393

Addictions treated:
Heroin, nicotine, alcohol, tranquillizers, caffeine, sugar.
Therapies used:
Acupuncture, aromatherapy, remedial massage, herbal medicine.
Cost:
Between £11 and £20 per consultation
Medicines: £2 per week.

Hampshire

The Basingstoke Clinic
18 Cliddesden Road, Basingstoke, Hampshire RG21 3DU
Tel: 0256 28128

Addictions treated:
Alcohol, nicotine, tranquillizers, sugar, caffeine.
Therapies used:
Acupuncture, homoeopathy, naturopathy, osteopathy.

Cost:
First consultation: £20 to £25
Subsequent treatments: Between £14 and £16.

Fareham Natural Health Centre
1 Hewlett Court, 30-32 West Street, Fareham, Hampshire.
Tel: 0329 285352

Addictions treated:
Alcohol, nicotine, tranquillizers, sugar, caffeine.
Therapies used:
Homoeopathy, nutrition and supplements, allergy tests.
Cost:
First consultation: £25
Subsequent consultations: £15
Reduced fees for children.

The Homoeopathic Clinic
13a North Street, Havant, Hampshire.
Tel: 0705 471757

Addictions treated:
Alcohol, nicotine, tranquillizers, sugar, caffeine.
Therapies used:
Homoeopathy, nutrition and supplements, allergy tests.
Cost:
First consultation: £25
Subsequent consultations: £15
Reduced fees for children.

The White Eagle Lodge
New Lands, Brewells Lane, Rake, Liss, Hampshire GU33 7HY
Tel: 0730 893300

Addictions treated:
All types.
Therapies used:
Absent healing, contact healing, use of directed colour rays.
Cost:
Donations only accepted.

The Homoeopathic Clinic
54 The Avenue, Southampton, Hampshire.
Tel: 0703 553748

Addictions treated:
Alcohol, nicotine, tranquillizers, sugar, caffeine.
Therapies used:
Homoeopathy, nutrition and supplements, allergy tests.
Cost:
First consultation: £25
Subsequent consultations: £15
Reduced fees for children.

The Centre for the Study of Complementary Medicine
51 Bedford Place, Southampton SO1 2DG
Tel: 0703 334752

Addictions treated:
(Heroin, cocaine and alcohol are treated only in conjunction
with a separate rehabilitation programme.)
Tranquillizers, nicotine, sugar, caffeine.
Therapies used:
Acupuncture, homoeopathy, herbal medicine, diet and
supplements.
Cost:
First consultation: £27
Subsequent consultations: £25

Herbal Treatment Centre
105 East Street, Southampton, Hampshire.
Tel: 0962 68776

Addictions treated:
Nicotine, tranquillizers, sugar.
Therapies used:
Medical herbalism, nutrition.
Cost:
First consultation: £25
Subsequent consultations: less, medicines extra.

Alternative Therapy Clinic
154 Shirley Road, Shirley, Southampton, Hampshire SO1 3FP
Tel: 0703 335054

Addictions treated:
Tranquillizers, sugar.
Therapy used:
Homoeopathy.
Cost:
£20 per 30-day course.

The Practitioners
80 Eling Lane, Eling, Totton, Hampshire SO4 4GG
Tel: 0703 861547

Addictions treated:
Alcohol, nicotine, tranquillizers, sugar.
Therapies used:
Hypnotherapy, psychotherapy, Bach flower remedies.
Cost:
First consultation: £15
Subsequent treatments: £10

Herbal Treatment Centre
41 Hatherley Road, Winchester, Hampshire.
Tel: 0962 68776

Addictions treated:
Nicotine, tranquillizers, sugar.
Therapies used:
Medical herbalism, nutrition.
Cost:
First consultation: £25
Subsequent consultations: less, medicines extra.

Herefordshire

Malvern Nature Cure Centre (residential)
5 College Grove, Great Malvern, Herefordshire and
Worcestershire WR14 3HP
Tel: 06845 66818

Addictions treated:
Nicotine, alcohol, tranquillizers, sugar, caffeine.

Therapies used:
Naturopathy, including nutrition, massage, water therapy, psychotherapy, exercise, relaxation, osteopathy.
Cost:
From £7 per day (bed and breakfast) upwards.

Hertfordshire

Wood Street Clinic
133 Wood Street, Barnet, Herts EN5 4BX
Tel: 01 441 0231 and 01 449 7656

Addictions treated:
Nicotine, alcohol, tranquillizers, sugar, caffeine.
Therapies used:
Acupuncture, hypnotherapy, nutrition, homoeopathy.
Cost:
Between £14 and £20 per session.

The Clinic
31 Heddon Court Avenue, Cockfosters, Barnet, Herts EN4 9NE
Tel: 01 449 4739

Addictions treated:
Tranquillizers, nicotine, alcohol, sugar.
Therapies used:
Hypnotherapy, counselling and psychotherapy.
Cost:
Between £15 and £25 a session.

The Practitioner
92 The Paddocks, Stevenage, Hertfordshire SG2 9UB
Tel: 0438 359632

Addictions treated:
Heroin, cocaine, nicotine, alcohol, tranquillizers, sugar, caffeine.
Therapies used:
Hypnotherapy, psychotherapy.
Cost:
£25 per session.

The Clinic
86 Handside Lane, Welwyn Garden City, Herts AL8 6SJ
Tel: 0707 320782

Addictions treated:
Tranquillizers, alcohol, nicotine, caffeine.
Therapies used:
Acupuncture, diet, herbal medicine, relaxation.
Cost:
First consultation: £25
Subsequent sessions: £12.50

Isles of Scilly

Natural Health Clinic
Jewel, Hill and Bennett, St Mary's, Isle of Scilly.
Tel: 0326 (Falmouth number) 318973

Addictions treated:
Tranquillizers, nicotine, alcohol, sugar, caffeine.
Therapy used:
Hypnotherapy.
Cost:
£25 per session.

Isle of Wight

The Hypnotherapy Consultancy
16 St Boniface Cliff Road, Shanklin, Isle of Wight.
Tel: 0983 862657

Addictions treated:
Nicotine, alcohol, tranquillizers, sugar.
Therapies used:
Hypnotherapy and counselling.
Cost:
Upon application.

Kent

Kent Natural Healing Clinic
Flat 6e, 26 Grimston Gardens, Folkestone, Kent CT20 2PX
Tel: 0303 46350

Addictions treated:
Alcohol, nicotine, sugar.
Therapy used:
Hypnotherapy.
Cost:
£10 per session

Maidstone Acupuncture Clinic
13 Boughton Lane, Loose, Maidstone, Kent ME15 9QN
Tel: 0622 41598

Addictions treated:
Heroin, nicotine, alcohol, tranquillizers, sugar, caffeine.
Therapies used:
Acupuncture, herbal medicine, bio-magnetics, nutrition,
supplements.
Cost:
£10 per session.

The Practitioner
9 Birtrick Drive, Meopham, Kent DA13 0LR
Tel: 0474 812135

Addictions treated:
Tranquillizers, alcohol, nicotine, sugar, caffeine.
Therapies used:

Osteopathy and cranial osteopathy, naturopathy, nutrition,
meditation techniques.
Cost:
First consultation £18
Subsequent treatments: £11

The College of Psycho-Therapeutics
'White Lodge', Stockland Green Road, Spendhurst, near
Tunbridge Wells, Kent TN3 0TT
Tel: 089286 3166

Addictions treated:
Heroin, alcohol, tranquillizers, nicotine, sugar, caffeine.
Therapies used:
Counselling, psychotherapy, healing.
Cost:
£10 per hour.

Please note that the College has a list of its trained counsellors working all over the country.

Herbal Treatment Centre
65 Frant Road, Tunbridge Wells, Kent TN2 5LH
Tel: 0892 27439

Addictions treated:
Heroin, cocaine, nicotine, alcohol, tranquillizers, sugar, caffeine.
Therapy used:
Medical herbalism.
Cost:
Please enquire.

The Practitioner
21 Granville Road, Tunbridge Wells, Kent TN1 2NU
Tel: 0892 21004

Addictions treated:
Nicotine, alcohol, tranquillizers, sugar, caffeine.
Therapies used:
Hypnotherapy, nutrition, Bach flower remedies, reflexology.
Cost:
£20 per session.

Metabolics Limited
Broadway House, 14 Mount Pleasant Road, Tunbridge Wells, Kent TN1 1QU
Tel: 0892 42609

Addictions treated:
Heroin, cocaine, nicotine, tranquillizers, caffeine, sugar.
Therapies used:
Nutrition (including amino acid therapy and other supplements), bio-energetic therapies.
Cost:
Whole treatment: £400 plus supplements.

The Practitioner
1 Sion Walk, Mount Sion, Tunbridge Wells, Kent.
Tel: 0892 23968

Addictions treated:
Tranquillizers, caffeine, sugar.
Therapies used:
Medical herbalism, diet, meditation, massage, counselling.
Cost:
£10 a session.

Lancashire

The Northwest Allergy Clinics
East Bank, New Church Road, Bolton, BL1 5QP, Lancashire,
and
Beaumont Hospital, Old Hall Clough, Bolton BL6 4LA
Tel: 0204 491869

Addictions treated:
Nicotine, sugar, caffeine.
Therapies used:
Neutralization technique, diet.
Cost:
Whole treatment: £600 to £800

Withnell Health Centre
Railway Road, Withnell, Chorley, Lancashire.
Tel: 0254 830311

Addiction treated:
Nicotine.
Therapies used:
Acupuncture, homoeopathy.
Cost:
£16 per session.

St Annes Remedial Clinic
33 Bromley Road, Lytham St Annes, Lancashire LY8 1PQ
Tel: 0253 727475

Addictions treated:
Nicotine, alcohol, tranquillizers, sugar.
Therapies used:
Ear acupuncture, allergy tests.
Cost:
Acupuncture: about £10
Allergy tests: about £35

Leicestershire

Ayurvedic Herbal Clinic
121 Coral Street, Leicester LE4 5BG
Tel: 0533 662475

Addictions treated:
Nicotine, caffeine.
Therapy used:
Ayurvedic medicine; an Indian approach using herbal and
homoeopathic medicine, acupressure and psychotherapy.
Cost:
£10 per session.

Ash-Shifa Clinic
446 East Park Road, Leicester, LE5 5HH
Tel: 0533 734633

Addiction treated:
Tranquillizers.
Therapies used:
Herbalism, psychotherapy, iridology.
Cost:
£15 per session including medicine.

Hydes Herbal Clinic
68 London Road, Leicester LE2 0QD
Tel: 0533 543178 and 543604

Addictions treated:
Tranquillizers, nicotine, alcohol, sugar, caffeine.
Therapy used:
Medical herbalism.
Cost:
First consultation: £10 to £20
Medicines: £4 to £5 a week.

Lincolnshire

Kesteven Natural Health Centre
Church Farm, Great Hale, Sleaford, Lincs NG34 9LL
Tel: 0529 60536

Addictions treated:

Heroin, cocaine, nicotine, alcohol, tranquillizers, alcohol, sugar, caffeine.
Therapies used:
Homoeopathy and radionics.
Cost:
Please enquire.

London

The Maisner Clinic
c/o City Health Centre, 36/37 Featherstone Street, London EC1Y 8QX
Tel: 01 251 4429

Addiction treated:
Sugar.
Therapies used:
Nutrition and supplements.
Cost:
£25 per consultation. Reduction for a course.

The Gestalt Centre
188 Old Street, London EC1V 9BP
Tel: For information please call 0727 (St Albans) 64806

Addictions treated:
Alcohol, sugar.
Therapy used:
Gestalt psychotherapy.
Cost:
Please enquire.

Community Health Foundation
188-194 Old Street, London EC1V 9BP
Tel: 01 251 4076

Addictions treated:
Tranquillizers, sugar, caffeine.
Therapies used:
Nutritional counselling, Shiatsu massage.
Cost:
£18 – £25 per session

Barbican Acupuncture Clinic
1 Wallside, Barbican, London EC2Y 8BJ
Tel: 01 628 5900/638 8200

Addictions treated:
Heroin, alcohol, nicotine, tranquillizers, caffeine.
Therapies used:
Acupuncture, nutrition, massage, herbal medicine.
Cost:
£15 per session.

The Private Polyclinic
142 Green Street, Forest Gate, London E7 8JQ
Tel: 01 472 0170

Addictions treated:
Nicotine, alcohol, tranquillizers, sugar, caffeine.
Therapies used:
Acupuncture, homoeopathy.
Cost:
Between £12 and £18 per session.

The Practitioner
Islington (London N1, address withheld by request)
Tel: 01 607 0341

Addictions treated:
Nicotine, alcohol, tranquillizers, sugar.
Therapies used:
Counselling, hypnotherapy, psychotherapy.
Cost:
£18 per hour.

Oasis Centre
72 Great North Road, East Finchley, London N2 0NL
Tel: 01 340 3924
Addictions treated:
Tranquillizers, nicotine, sugar, caffeine.
Therapies used:
Hypnotherapy, Gestalt psychotherapy, counselling, Bach flower
remedies, Touch for Health.
Cost:
First consultation: £25
Subsequent consultations: £15

Finchley Alternative Medical Centre
253 Ballards Lane, Finchley, London N3
Tel: 01 445 2631

Addictions treated:
Heroin, cocaine, nicotine, alcohol, tranquillizers, sugar,
caffeine.
Therapy used:
Acupuncture in the form of moratherapy (a kind of electro-
acupuncture).
Cost:
First consultation £25
Subsequent consultations: £15

Highgate Natural Health Centre
213 Archway Road, London N6
Tel: 01 341 2769

Addictions treated:
Tranquillizers, alcohol, nicotine, sugar, caffeine.
Therapies used:
Medical herbalism, nutrition, homoeopathy, massage,
meditation, exercise.
Cost:
First consultation: £13
Subsequent treatments: £7 (medication extra)

The Practitioner
1c Harold Road, London N8 7DE
Tel: 01 341 6539

Addictions treated:
Heroin, alcohol, nicotine, tranquillizers.
Therapies used:
Hypnotherapy, relaxation.
Cost:
£20 per session.

The Clinic
213c Woodhouse Road, Finchley, London N12 9AY
Tel: 01 361 2293

Addictions treated:
Nicotine, alcohol, tranquillizers, caffeine.

Nicotine, alcohol, tranquillizers, caffeine.
Therapies used:
Acupuncture, nutrition, counselling.
Cost:
£14 per consultation.

Clissold Park Natural Health Centre
154 Church Street, London N16 0JU
Tel: 01 249 2990

Addictions treated:
Heroin, cocaine, tranquillizers, nicotine, alcohol, sugar.
Therapies used:
Homoeopathy, nutrition.
Cost:
First consultation (one-and-a-half hours): £18
Subsequent consultations: £15

Isis Alternative Health Resources
362 High Road, London N17
Tel: 01 808 6401

Addictions treated:
Nicotine, heroin, tranquillizers, caffeine.
Therapies used:
Acupuncture, nutrition and supplements, counselling and
psychotherapy, DMA creative skill building (a psychological
technique).
Cost:
£15 per consultation.

Acu Medic Centre
101-103 Camden High Street, London NW1 7JN
Tel: 01 388 5783

Addictions treated:
Heroin, alcohol, nicotine, tranquillizers, caffeine.
Therapies used:
Acupuncture, homoeopathy.
Cost:
£16 per session.

Transcendental Meditation Centre, 24 Linhope Street, London
NW1 6HT
Tel: 01 402 3451

The Core Trust
7 Lisson Cottages, Lisson Grove, London NW1 6UD
Tel: 01 258 3031

Addictions treated:
Heroin, cocaine, tranquillizers, nicotine, alcohol, sugar.
Therapies recommended:
(The Trust is a referral agency; there are no practitioners on the
premises.) Acupuncture, homoeopathy, counselling and
psychotherapy, hypnotherapy, reflexology, nutrition, healing,
exercise, relaxation.
Cost: Please enquire.

The Alternative and Orthodox Medicine Clinic
PO Box 598, 56 Harley House, Marylebone Road, London
NW1 5HW
Tel: 01 486 4115

Addictions treated:
Nicotine, alcohol, sugar, tranquillizers.
Therapy used:
Hypnotherapy.
Cost:
£25 per session.

Hypnotherapy Centre
28 Rochester Square, London NW1
Tel: 01 267 2208

Addictions treated:
Nicotine, tranquillizers.
Therapy used:
Hypnotherapy.
Cost:
£25 per session.

The Centre for the Study of Complementary Medicine
6 Upper Harley Street, London NW1
Tel: 01 935 7848

Addictions treated:
Heroin, cocaine and alcohol are treated only in conjunction with
a separate rehabilitation programme. Tranquillizers,
nicotine,sugar, caffeine addictions are also treated.

Therapies used:
Acupuncture, homoeopathy, herbal medicine, diet and supplements.
Cost:
First consultation: £40
Subsequent consultations: £30

The Clinic
53 Shirlock Road, London NW3 2HR
Tel: 01 267 8448

Addictions treated:
Heroin, cocaine, nicotine, alcohol, tranquillizers, sugar, caffeine.
Therapies used:
Acupuncture, osteopathy and cranial osteopathy.
Cost:
First consultation: £18
Subsequent consultations: £15

The Clinic
11 Alderton Crescent, Hendon, London NW4 3XU
Tel: 01 202 6242

Addictions treated:
Alcohol, tranquillizers, nicotine, sugar, caffeine.
Therapies used:
Nutrition, acupuncture, osteopathy and cranial osteopathy, homoeopathy, herbal medicine, supplements, counselling.
Cost:
First consultation: £36
Subsequent treatments: £30

The Clinic
167 Victoria Road, London NW6
Tel: 01 624 1050

Addictions treated:
Cocaine, heroin, alcohol, tranquillizers, nicotine, sugar, caffeine.
Therapies used:
Homoeopathy, acupuncture, counselling, diet.

Cost:
First consultation: Three-and-a-half hours: £30 (Full medical history.)
Subsequent treatments: Between £15 and £22

Acupuncture Centre
60 Tranquil Vale, Blackheath, London SE3
Tel: 01 318 3849

Addictions treated:
Heroin, nicotine, alcohol, sugar, caffeine.
Therapy used:
Acupuncture.
Cost:
£15 per session.

College of Homoeopathy Clinic
26 Clarendon Rise, Lewisham, London SE13
Tel: 01 852 0573

Addictions treated:
Heroin, cocaine, nicotine, alcohol, tranquillizers, sugar, caffeine.
Therapy used:
Homoeopathy.
Cost:
First consultation: £20
Subsequent consultations: £12

The Clinic
58 Edison Grove, London SE18 2DN
Tel: 01 854 4632

Addictions treated:
Alcohol, nicotine, tranquillizers.
Therapy used:
Hypnotherapy.
Cost:
Between £17 and £22 a session.

The Practitioner
95 Bovill Road, Forest Hill, London SE23 1EL
Tel: 01 291 5466

Addictions treated:
Heroin, cocaine, nicotine.
Therapies used:
Acupuncture, massage, reflexology, iridology (diagnosis by examination of the eyes), relaxation, counselling.
Cost:
£15 per session.

The Practitioner
119 South Norwood Hill, London SE25 6DD
Tel: 01 653 6931

Addiction treated:
Nicotine.
Therapies used:
Hypnotherapy, counselling.
Cost:
£25 per session.

The Practitioner
12 Halsey Street, London SW3
Tel: 01 584 0957

Addictions treated:
Heroin, alcohol.
Therapies used:
Healing, counselling.
Cost:Please enquire.

The Clapham Common Clinic
First floor, 151-153 Clapham High Street, London SW4
Tel: 01 622 4382/627 8890

Addictions treated:
Alcohol, nicotine, tranquillizers, cocaine, caffeine.
Therapies used:
Acupuncture, homoeopathy, osteopathy.
Cost:
First consultation: £25
Subsequent treatments: £15

The South London Natural Health Centre
7a Clapham Common Southside, London SW4
Tel: 01 720 8817

Addictions treated:
Nicotine, tranquillizers, alcohol, sugar, cocaine.
Therapies used:
Hypnotherapy, homoeopathy, acupuncture, naturopathy,
polarity therapy, nutrition, aromatherapy, counselling and
psychotherapy, flotation tank with audio tapes.
Cost:
Between £10 and £20 per session.

Hypnotherapy Practice
74 Halford Road, London SW6 1JX
Tel: 01 385 1166

Addictions treated:
Nicotine, alcohol, heroin, cocaine, tranquillizers, sugar,
caffeine.
Therapies used:
Hypnotherapy and psychotherapy, counselling.
Cost:
£12 per session.

The Practitioner
21 Thurloe Place, London SW7 2DP
Tel: Please call 0799 26138 for all information and
appointments.

Addictions treated:
Heroin, cocaine, nicotine, alcohol, tranquillizers, sugar,
caffeine.
Therapies used:
Iridology (diagnosis by examination of the eyes), herbal
medicine, homoeopathy, naturopathy, nutrition, Bach flower
remedies.
Cost:
First consultation: £20
Subsequent consultations: £15

The Healing Clinic
15 Ann Lane, London SW10
Tel: 01 351 1457

Addictions treated:
Heroin, cocaine, tranquillizers, alcohol.

Therapies used:
Healing, both laying on of hands and absent healing, with counselling.
Cost:
Donations only.

The Natural Healing Centre
35 Observatory Road, East Sheen, London SW14 7QB
Tel: 01 878 7579
Addictions treated:
Nicotine, alcohol, tranquillizers, caffeine, sugar.
Therapies used:
Hypnotherapy and acupuncture.
Cost:
First consultation: £22
Subsequent consultations: £14

The Practitioner
14 Brandlehow Road, Putney, London SW15 2ED
Tel: 01 874 2414

Addictions treated:
Sugar, caffeine.
Therapy used:
Nutrition and supplements.
Cost:
First consultation: £15 to £25
Subsequent consultations: £10 to £15

Putney Natural Therapy Clinic
11 Montserrat Road, Putney, London SW15 2LD
Tel: 01 789 2548

Addiction treated:
Alcohol.
Therapies used:
Acupuncture, naturopathy, homoeopathy, hypnotherapy, diet.
Cost:
Between £15 and £20 per consultation.

The Practitioner
26 Rayners Road, Putney, London SW15 2AZ
Tel: 01 788 4126/785 3564

Addictions treated:
Nicotine, alcohol, tranquillizers, caffeine, sugar.
Therapies used:
Hypnotherapy, counselling, relaxation.
Cost:
£10 per session.

Teleos Clinic
9 Cavendish Square, London W1
Tel: 01 637 3088

Addiction treated:
Tranquillizers.
Therapies used:
Herbal medicine, aromatherapy, nutrition.
Cost:
Between £17 and £25 a treatment.

The Practitioner
26 Wendover Court, Chiltern Street, London W1
Tel: 01 486 4553

Addictions treated:
Tranquillizers, alcohol, nicotine, caffeine, sugar.
Therapy used:
Hypnotherapy.
Cost:
£30 per session.

Hypno-Analysis Centre of West London
31 Harley Street, London W1N 1DA
Tel: 01 580 7576

Addictions treated:
Nicotine, alcohol, heroin, sugar, caffeine.
Therapies used:
Hypnotherapy, homoeopathy.
Cost:
Tobacco: £50 for a consultation, with free treatments if needed
during the following month
Hypnoanalysis: Between £17 and £35 per session
Tests: please enquire

Holistic Health Centre
138 Harley Street, London W1N 1AH
Tel: 01 935 0554 or 01 202 3800

Addictions treated:
Heroin, nicotine, alcohol, tranquillizers, sugar, caffeine.
Therapies used:
Acupuncture, nutrition and supplements, homoeopathy,
meditation, relaxation.
Cost:
First consultation: £45
Subsequent sessions: £20
Medicines and further tests extra.

Academy of Hypnotherapy and Professional Hypnotherapist
Centre
181 Cat Hill, Cockfosters, Herts EN4 8HJ
Tel: 01 441 9685
Consulting Rooms:
Harley Street, London W1

Addictions treated:
Alcohol, tranquillizers, sugar, caffeine.
Therapies used:
Hypnotherapy and psychotherapy.
Cost:
£35 per session.

London Medical Centre
144 Harley Street, London W1N 1AH
Tel: 01 935 0023

Addictions treated:
Nicotine, tranquillizers, alcohol, sugar.
Therapies used:
Nutrition and supplements, acupuncture, hypnotherapy.
Cost:
First consultation: between £50 and £75
Subsequent consultations less.

The Hale Clinic
7 Park Crescent, London W1N 3HE
Tel: 01 631 0156

Addictions treated:
Nicotine, alcohol, tranquillizers, sugar, caffeine.
Therapies used:
Homoeopathy, acupuncture, medical herbalism.
Cost:
Between £18 and £45 per consultation.

The Clinic
51 Queen Anne Street, London W1M 9FA
Tel: 01 935 7075

Addictions treated:
Alcohol, nicotine, tranquillizers.
Therapy used:
Hypnotherapy.
Cost:
Between £17 and £22 a session.

The Clinic
101 Seymour Place, London W1H 5TG
Tel: 01 262 4507

Addictions treated:
Cocaine, nicotine, alcohol, tranquillizers, sugar, caffeine.
Therapies used:
Homoeopathy, nutrition and supplements, herbal medicine,
acupuncture, counselling.
Cost:
Between £250 and £500 per week.

Centre for Health and Healing
St James's Church, 197 Piccadilly, London W1V 9LF
Tel: 01 437 7118

Addictions treated:
Alcohol, tranquillizers, sugar, caffeine.
Therapies used:
Counselling, psychotherapy, healing, homoeopathy,
acupuncture, massage, osteopathy, self-care programme.
Cost:
Sliding scale to a maximum of £15 per session

Neal's Yard Therapy Rooms
2 Neal's Yard, Covent Garden, London WC2H 9DP
Tel: 01 379 7662

Addictions treated:
Heroin, cocaine, nicotine, alcohol, tranquillizers, sugar,
caffeine.
Therapies used:
Acupuncture, Alexander technique, applied kinesology (touch
therapy), aromatherapy, Bach flower remedies, biofeedback,
cranial osteopathy, healing, medical herbalism, homoeopathy,
massage, nutrition, naturopathy, psychotherapy, reflexology, etc.
Cost:
Between £12 and £20 per consultation.

Bayswater Allergy Clinic
25b Clanricarde Gardens, London W2 4JL
Tel: 01 229 9078

Addictions treated:
Alcohol, nicotine, tranquillizers, sugar, caffeine.
Therapies used:
Allergy tests, desensitization, diet, supplements.
Cost:
Consultation and tests: £50
Initial treatment and supplements £110

The Gerda Boyesen Clinic
Acacia House, Centre Avenue, Acton Park, London W3 7JX
Tel: 01 743 2437

Addictions treated:
Heroin, cocaine, nicotine, alcohol, tranquillizers, sugar,
caffeine.
Therapies used:
Massage, psychotherapy, counselling (Biodynamic Psychiatry
and Biodynamic Psychotherapy).
Cost:
First half-hour consultation: £10
Subsequent 50-minute treatments: £20

The London Natural Health Clinic
Arnica House, 170 Campden Hill Road, London W8 7AS
Tel: 01 938 3788

Addictions treated:
Heroin, cocaine, nicotine, alcohol, tranquillizers, sugar, caffeine.
Therapies used:
Acupuncture, hypnotherapy, naturopathy.
Cost:
First consultation: £25
Subsequent consultations: Between £15 and £25
Allergy tests: Between £15 and £30

The Practitioner
Flat 11, 18 Ladbroke Square, London W11 3NA
Tel: 01 221 9245

Addictions treated:
Nicotine, tranquillizers, sugar, caffeine.
Therapies used:
Counselling, nutrition with supplements, remedial massage, reflexology, colour therapy, yoga with relaxation and meditation, healing.
Cost:
£25 an hour
Small groups: £3.50 to £5 per person.

Centre for Counselling and Psychotherapy Education
21 Lancaster Road, London W11 1QL
Tel: 01 221 3215

Addictions treated:
Heroin, cocaine, alcohol.
Therapy used:
Psychotherapy.
Cost:
£3 per session (supervised student practitioner).
£15

Manchester

US Homoeopathic Clinic
1029 Stockport Road, Levenshulme, Manchester M19 2TB
Tel: 061 442 8861

Addictions treated:
Alcohol, tranquillizers.

Therapy used:
Homoeopathy.
Cost:
First consultation and prescription: £25
Subsequent consultations and prescriptions: £17

Women's Clinic
9 Hall Lane, Manchester M23 8AQ
Tel: 061 998 5711

Addictions treated:
Tranquillizers, alcohol.
Therapies used:
Counselling, relaxation, meditation.
Cost:
No charge.

The Other Clinic
81 Palatine Road, Withington, Manchester M20 9LJ
Tel: 061 434 5075

Addictions treated:
Nicotine, alcohol, cocaine, heroin, caffeine, sugar.
Therapies used:
Homoeopathy, nutrition, acupuncture, healing.
Cost:

Merseyside

The Clinic
6 Rodney Street, Liverpool L1 2TE
Tel: 051 709 1745

Addictions treated:
Heroin, cocaine, nicotine, tranquillizers, alcohol, caffeine,
sugar.
Therapies used:
Homoeopathy, acupuncture, hypnotherapy, nutrition,
Alexander technique (postural re-education), exercise,
psychotherapy and counselling.
Cost:
Between £9 and £40 per session.

The Clinic
12 Rodney Street, Liverpool L1 2TE
Tel: 051 709 0479

Addictions treated:
Nicotine, alcohol, tranquillizers.
Therapies used:
Acupuncture, herbal medicine, massage, counselling.
Cost:
Between £8.50 and £10.50 per treatment.
Medicines: £2.50 for 2 weeks' supply.

Shire Herbal Clinic
14 Rodney Street, Liverpool L1 2TE
Tel: 051 709 4261

Addictions treated:
Nicotine, alcohol, sugar, caffeine.
Therapies used:
Herbal medicine, iridology (diagnosis from the iris of the eyes),
nutrition, counselling.
Cost:
Initial consultation and 4 weeks' treatment: £25
Subsequent consultations and 4 weeks' treatment: £14.50

The Society of Biophysical Medicine Acupuncture Drug Clinic
New Zealand House, 18 Water Street, Liverpool L2 8TD
Tel: 051 227 3333

Addictions treated:
Heroin, nicotine, tranquillizers
Therapy used:
Electro-acupuncture.
Cost:
No charge.

Middlesex

Edgware Centre for Natural Health
128 High Street, Edgware, Middlesex HA8 7EL
Tel: 01 951 3475 or 01 952 9566

Addictions treated:
Heroin, cocaine, nicotine, alcohol, tranquillizers, sugar,
caffeine.

Therapies used:
Acupuncture, homoeopathy, medical herbalism.
Cost:
Between £12 and £20 per session.

The Clinic of Acupuncture
36 Park Grove, Edgware, Middlesex HA8 8SJ
Tel: 01 958 9657

Addictions treated:
Heroin, alcohol, nicotine, tranquillizers, caffeine.
Therapies used:
Acupuncture, relaxation, massage.
Cost:
£15 per treatment.
£12 for old age pensioners.

Hampton Osteopathic Clinic
87 High Street, Hampton, Middlesex
Tel: 01 979 3119

Addictions treated:
Nicotine, tranquillizers, alcohol, sugar, caffeine.
Therapies used:
Homoeopathy, cranial osteopathy, medical herbalism,
acupuncture, reflexology, nutrition, counselling.
Cost:
First consultation: £20
Subsequent consultations: £17

The Natural Healing Centre
1a New Pond Parade, West End Road, Ruislip Gardens,
Ruislip, Middlesex HA4 6LR
Tel: 0895 675464

Addictions treated:
Heroin, cocaine, nicotine, alcohol, tranquillizers, sugar,
caffeine.
Therapies used:
Homoeopathy, radionics, ortho-bionomy, pulsors, colour,
natural healing, allergy testing, psychotherapy, reflexology,
hypnosis, Bach flower remedies.
Cost:
Between £12 and £20 per consultation.

The Practitioner
33 Westholme Gardens, Ruislip, Middlesex HA4 8QJ
Tel: 0895 633753

Addictions treated:
Nicotine, alcohol, tranquillizers, sugar.
Therapy used:
Hypnotherapy.
Cost:
First consultation: £29 for one-and-a-half hours.
Subsequent consultation: £24 each for one hour.

Norfolk

The Clinic
93 High Road, Gorleston, Great Yarmouth, Norfolk NR31 0PE
Tel: 0493 650044

This clinic has only recently opened, but its practitioners will be
happy to treat any drug addiction.
Therapies used:
Acupuncture, osteopathy, reflexology.
Cost:
Examination: £20
Treatment: £12

The Complementary Medicine Centre
Sackville Place, 44/48 Magdalen Street, Norwich NR3 1JE
Tel: 0603 616221/633933

Addictions treated:
Nicotine, alcohol, tranquillizers, sugar, caffeine.
Therapies used:
Hypnotherapy, psychotherapy and counselling, nutrition,
massage, reflexology.
Cost:
Between £20 and £25 per session.

Alderbury Clinic of Traditional Acupuncture
48 Whitehall Road, Norwich, Norfolk NR2 3EW
Tel: 0603 663186

This clinic has only recently opened, but its practitioners will be
happy to treat any drug addiction.

Therapy used:
Acupuncture.
Cost:
Examination: £20
Treatment: £12

Oxfordshire

The Banbury Clinic of Traditional Acupuncture
32 Crouch Street, Banbury, Oxfordshire OX16 9PR
Tel: 0295 3726

Addictions treated:
Tranquillizers, nicotine, sugar, caffeine.
Therapies used:
Acupuncture, Bach flower remedies.
Cost:
Consultations: £20
Treatments: £12

The Oxford Acupuncture Centre
41 Walton Crescent, Jericho, Oxford OX1 2JQ
Tel: 0865 54631

Addictions treated:
Heroin, cocaine, nicotine, alcohol, tranquillizers, sugar,
caffeine.
Therapy used:
Acupuncture.
Cost:
First consultation: £22
Subsequent treatments: £12

The Clinic of Natural Medicine
Virginia Cottage, Nether Westcote, Kingham, Oxfordshire.
Tel: 0993 830419

Addictions treated:
Heroin, nicotine, alcohol, tranquillizers, caffeine, sugar.
Therapies used:
Acupuncture, aromatherapy, remedial massage, herbal
medicine.
Cost:
First consultation: £20

Subsequent treatments: £11
Acupuncture: £11
Medicines: about £2 per week.

The Park End Clinic
9 Park End Street, Oxford
Tel: 0865 251055

Addictions treated:
Nicotine, alcohol, tranquillizers, sugar.
Therapies used:
Hypnotherapy, psychotherapy.
Cost:
£24 per session.

The Practitioner
18 Mayfield Avenue, Grove, near Wantage, Oxfordshire
OX12 7LZ
Tel: 02357 65936

Addictions treated:
Nicotine, alcohol, tranquillizers, sugar.
Therapies used:
Hypnotherapy, psychotherapy.
Cost:
Consultations: £10
Treatments: £15

The Complementary Therapy Centre
37 Wallingford Street, Wantage, Oxfordshire OX12 8AU
Tel: 02357 67698

Addictions treated:
Nicotine, alcohol, tranquillizers, sugar, caffeine.
Therapies used:
Counselling, hypnotherapy, Bach flower remedies.
Cost:
£20 per session.

The Witney Clinic
Church Green, Witney, Oxon OX8 6YR
Tel: 0993 73567

Addictions treated:

Nicotine, tranquillizers, sugar, caffeine.
Therapies used:
Acupuncture, homoeopathy, hypnotherapy.
Cost:
Between £14 and £21 per session.

Shropshire

Newport Clinic of Acupuncture and Preventive Medicine
4 Abbey Court, High Street, Newport, Shropshire TP10 7BE
Tel: 0952 813219

Addictions treated:
Nicotine, tranquillizers, sugar, caffeine.
Therapies used:
Acupuncture and clinical kinesiology.
Cost:
£6 to £10 per session.

St Oswald's Centre for Holistic Healing
22 Upper Brook Street, Oswestry, Shropshire SY11 2TB
Tel: 0691 655470

Addictions treated:
Alcohol, tranquillizers, sugar, caffeine.
Therapies used:
Acupuncture, medical herbalism, diet, healing, reflexology,
radionics, osteopathy, homoeopathy.
Cost:
First consultations: Between £15 and £22
Subsequent consultations: Between £10 and £15

The Acupuncture Clinic
Aston Rogers, Westbury, Shropshire SY5 9HQ
Tel: 074383 422

Addictions treated:
Tranquillizers, nicotine, caffeine.
Therapies used:
Acupuncture, psychotherapy, herbal medicine, relaxation,
visualization.
Cost:
First consultation of two hours: £24
Subsequent treatments: £12

Somerset

The Allergy Analysis Service
20 Taunton Road, Pedwell, Bridgwater, Somerset TA7 9BG
Tel: 0458 210425

Addictions treated:
Tranquillizers, sugar, caffeine.
Therapies used:
Radionics (medical dowsing), nutrition, homoeopathy, allergy testing.
Cost:
Initial test £10, including six weeks' advice.

The Practitioner
Ben Knowle, Worth, near Wells, Somerset BA5 1LW
Tel: 0749 75352

Addictions treated:
Tranquillizers, alcohol, nicotine, sugar, caffeine.
Therapy used:
Medical herbalism.
Cost:Please enquire.

The Natural Healing Centre
Coombe Valley, Eastwell Lane, Winscombe, Somerset
BS25 1DA
Tel: 093484 3782

Addictions treated:
Tranquillizers, sugar, caffeine.
Therapies used:
Herbal medicine, nutrition, healing, counselling, Bach flower remedies.
Cost:
First consultation: £25
Subsequent consultations: £12
Medicines: about £18 a month.

The Clinic of Complementary Medicine
40a Princes Street, Yeovil, Somerset BA20 1EQ
Tel: 0935 22488

Addictions treated:
Heroin, tranquillizers, alcohol, nicotine, caffeine.

Therapy used:
Acupuncture
Cost:
First consultation: £24 for one-and-a-half hours
Subsequent treatments: £12

Staffordshire

The Natural Health and Iridology Centre
19 Park Terrace, Tunstall, Stoke-on-Trent, Staffordshire
ST6 6PB
Tel: 0782 819855

Addictions treated:
Nicotine, alcohol.
Therapies used:
Medical herbalism, iridology (diagnosis by examination of the
eye), water treatment.
Cost:
£14 to £28 per consultation.

Alternative Therapy Centre
25 Lower Gungate, Tamworth, Staffordshire B79 7AT
Tel: 0827 68374

Addictions treated:
Heroin, cocaine, nicotine, alcohol, tranquillizers, sugar,
caffeine.
Therapies used:
Acupuncture, herbal medicine, hypnotherapy.
Cost:
Between £11 and £14 per session.

Suffolk

The Paul Lambillion Clinic
27 Abbotsbury Road, Bury St Edmunds, Suffolk IP33 2HN
Tel: 0284 64780

Addiction treated:
Tranquillizers.
Therapies used:
Healing, visualization and meditation, breathing, relaxation,

exercise, homoeopathy, nutrition, singing, painting and drawing, massage.
Cost:
£10 per session.

The Paul Lambillion Clinic
The Sanctuary, 'Woodcrest', Great Saxham, near Bury St Edmunds, Suffolk
Tel: 0284 64780

Addiction treated:
Tranquillizers.
Therapies used:
Healing, visualization and meditation, breathing, relaxation, exercise, homoeopathy, nutrition, singing, painting and drawing, massage.
Cost:
£10 per session.

East Anglian School of Shiatsu
2 Capondale Cottages, New Lane, Holbrook, Ipswich, Suffolk
IP9 2RB
Tel: 0473 328061

Addictions treated:
Alcohol, tranquillizers, sugar, caffeine.
Therapies used:
Shiatsu, Macrobiotic dietary guidance, counselling.
Cost:
First one-and-a-half hour session: £14
Subsequent one hour sessions: £10

The Practitioner
521 Foxhall Road, Ipswich, Suffolk. IP3 8LW
Tel: 0473 73552

Addictions treated:
Nicotine, sugar, caffeine.
Therapies used:
Acupuncture, nutrition.
Cost:
First consultation: £15
Subsequent consultations: £10

The Practitioner
240 Sidegate Lane, Ipswich, Suffolk
Tel: 0473 726906

Addictions treated:
Tranquillizers, alcohol, nicotine, sugar, caffeine.
Therapies used:
Medical herbalism, nutrition, homoeopathy, massage,
meditation, exercise.
Cost:
First consultation: £12
Subsequent treatments: £6 plus medication.

Lowestoft Clinic of Traditional Acupuncture
Halliday's Chemist, 48 London Road North, Lowestoft,
Suffolk.
Tel: 0502 3126

This clinic has only recently opened, but its practitioners will be
happy to treat any drug addiction.
Therapy used:
Acupuncture.
Cost:
Examination: £20
Treatment: £12

The Clinic
Thornham Herb Garden, Thornham Magna, near Eye, Suffolk
IP23 8HA
Tel: 0379 83510

Addictions treated:
Nicotine, alcohol, tranquillizers, sugar, caffeine.
Therapies used:
Nutrition, supplements, herbal medicine, water treatments,
counselling.
Cost:
£20 per hour.

Surrey

Epsom Clinic of Homoeopathy
8 Craddocks Parade, Ashtead, Surrey KT21 1QL
Tel: 03727 21706 and 03722 78477

Addictions treated:
Nicotine, alcohol, tranquillizers, caffeine, sugar.
Therapy used:
Homoeopathy.
Cost:
First consultation: £25
Subsequent consultations: £15

Clinic
Filebrook, 12 Pixham Lane, Dorking, Surrey RH4 1PT
Telephone number withheld on request.

Addictions treated:
Tranquillizers, alcohol.
Therapy used:
Nutrition, using clinical ecology and allergy testing,
supplements.
Cost:
£15 per hour.

The Practitioner
4 Hallam Road, Godalming, Surrey
Tel: 04868 29183

Addictions treated:
Tranquillizers, tobacco, caffeine, sugar.
Therapies used:
Homoeopathy, nutrition.
Cost:
First consultation: £17
Subsequent treatments: £10

The Clinic
4 Waterden Road, Guildford, Surrey
Tel: 0483 503240

Addictions treated:
Alcohol, nicotine, tranquillizers, sugar, caffeine.
Therapies used:
Homoeopathy, nutrition, massage, relaxation, counselling.
Cost:
First consultation: £40
Subsequent consultations: £15

The Kingston Clinic of Physiotherapy and Alternative
Therapies
228 Richmond Road, Kingston upon Thames, Surrey
KT2 5HG
Tel: 01 546 4513

Addictions treated:
Alcohol, nicotine, sugar, caffeine.
Therapies used:
Neuro-electric therapy (based on acupuncture), homoeopathy,
diet.
Cost:
First consultation: £20
Subsequent consultations: £18

Edwards Health Centre
59 Blakes Lane, New Malden, Surrey
Tel: 01 949 4572

Addiction treated:
Nicotine
Therapy used: hypnotherapy
Cost:
Consultations: £12 each.
Consultation plus two treatments: £62

The Clinic
Lark Rise, Franks Field, Peaslake, Dorking, Surrey
Tel: 0384 503240

Addictions treated:
Alcohol, nicotine, tranquillizers, sugar, caffeine.
Therapies used:
Homoeopathy, nutrition, massage, relaxation, counselling.
Cost:
First consultation: £40
Subsequent consultations: £15

The Practitioner
61 Eastnor Road, Reigate, Surrey RH2 8NE
Tel: 0737 221366

Addictions treated:
Tranquillizers, nicotine, sugar, caffeine, may take on heroin and alcohol.
Therapies used:
Homoeopathy, healing, reflexology, massage.
Cost:
First consultation: £30
Subsequent consultations: £15

The Clinic
39 Browne Road, Surbiton, Surrey KT3 8ST
Tel: 01 399 3215

Addictions treated:
Nicotine, alcohol, tranquillizers, sugar, caffeine.
Therapy used:
Applied kinesiology, or Touch for Health.
Cost:
First treatment: £25
Subsequent treatments: £15

The Practitioner
19 Blanchmans Road, Warlingham, Surrey CR3 9DF
Tel: 08832 4855

Addictions treated:
Nicotine, alcohol, tranquillizers, sugar, caffeine.
Therapy used:
Hypnotherapy.
Cost:
£15 per session.

Sussex

Gaia Natural Therapies
London Road, Forest Row, East Sussex RH18 5EZ
Tel: 0342 822716

Addictions treated:
Nicotine, tranquillizers, sugar.
Therapies used:
Nutrition, acupuncture, hypnotherapy.

Cost:
£14 per session.

The Practitioner
Stream Cottage, Wish Hill, Willingdon, East Sussex
BH20 9HQ
Tel: 0323 510540

Addictions treated:
Nicotine, alcohol, tranquillizers.
Therapy used:
Hypnotherapy.
Cost:
Between £30 and £100 for a course of treatment.

Chichester Acupuncture Clinic
128 Parklands Road, Chichester, Sussex PO19 3EB
Tel: 0243 778159

Addictions treated:
Nicotine, tranquillizers.
Therapy used:
Acupuncture.
Cost:
First consultation: £20
Subsequent consultations: £15

Clinic
'Moonrakers', Blackness Road, Crowborough, Sussex
TN6 2LP
Tel: 08926 5195

Addictions treated:
Nicotine, alcohol, tranquillizers, sugar, caffeine.,
Therapy used:
Psychotherapy.
Cost:
£10 for two hours (group session).
£20 for 50 minutes (individual session).

The Practitioner
230 Seven Sisters Road, Lower Willingdon, Eastbourne, Susse
BN22 OPG
Tel: 0323 502693

Addictions treated:
Nicotine, tranquillizers, alcohol, sugar.
Therapy used:
Hypnotherapy.
Cost:
£15 per session.

The Practitioner
83 Ham Road, East Worthing, Sussex
Tel: 0903 207708

Addictions treated:
Heroin, nicotine, alcohol, tranquillizers, caffeine.
Therapies used:
Hypnotherapy, psychotherapy, relaxation.
Cost:
£15 per session.

The International College of Oriental Medicine UK Limited
Clinic
Green Hedges House, Green Hedges Avenue, East Grinstead,
Sussex RH19 1DZ
Tel: 0342 313106

Addictions treated:
Nicotine, tranquillizers, sugar, caffeine.
Therapies used:
Acupuncture, nutrition.
Cost:
First treatment: £16
Subsequent treatments: £12

The Maisner Centre for Eating Disorders
PO Box 464, Hove, Sussex BN3 2BN
Tel: 0273 729818/29334

Addiction treated:
Sugar.
Therapy used:
Nutrition and supplements, relaxation.
Cost:
£25 per consultation.
Reduction for a course.

The Wilbury Clinic of Natural Medicine
64 Wilbury Road, Hove, Sussex BH3 3PY
Tel: 0273 24420 and 26777

Addictions treated:
Heroin, cocaine, nicotine, alcohol, tranquillizers, sugar,
caffeine.
Therapies used:
Medical herbalism, acupuncture, nutrition.
Cost:
Between £15 and £25 per consultation.

The Practitioner
29 Bath Road, Worthing, Sussex
Tel: 0903 38612

Addictions treated:
Nicotine, alcohol, tranquillizers, sugar, caffeine.
Therapies used:
Hypnotherapy, psychotherapy and counselling.
Cost:
£24 per session.

The Practitioner
46 West Street, Chichester, West Sussex PO19 1RP
Tel: 0243 786652/527800

Addictions treated:
Nicotine, tranquillizers, sugar, caffeine.
Therapies used:
Hypnotherapy and psychotherapy.
Cost:
£20 per session.

Horsham Natural Health Centre
76 Park Street, Horsham, West Sussex RH12 1DX
Tel: 0403 57328

Addictions treated:
Nicotine, alcohol, sugar, tranquillizers.
Therapy used:
Hypnotherapy.
Cost:
£25 per session.

Tyne and Wear

The Practitioner
9 Bedeburn Road, Whorlton Grange, Westerhope, Newcastle,
NE5 4JL
Tel: 091 286 1161

Addictions treated:
Heroin, cocaine, nicotine, alcohol, tranquillizers, sugar,
caffeine.
Therapies used:
Psychotherapy, counselling, hypnotherapy.
Cost:
First consultation free.
Subsequent sessions: £14

The Practitioner
35 Valley Forge, Washington, Tyne and Wear NE38 7JN
Tel: 091 416 7324

Addictions treated:
Nicotine, tranquillizers, alcohol, sugar, caffeine.
Therapies used:
Hypnotherapy, psychotherapy.
Cost:
First consultation: free
Subsequent treatments: £13
(For tobacco, £25 for a 2-week course)

West Midlands

Birmingham Relaxation and Fitness Centre
8 Balaclava Road, Kings Heath, Birmingham B14 7SG
Tel: 021 444 5435

Addictions treated, in consultation with the South Birmingham
Hypnotherapy Centre at the same address:
Heroin, cocaine, nicotine, alcohol, tranquillizers, sugar,
caffeine.
Therapy used:
Deep relaxation massage.
Cost:
£17 per session.

South Birmingham Hypnotherapy Centre
8 Balaclava Road, Kings Heath, Birmingham B14 7SG
Tel: 021 444 5435

Addictions treated:
Heroin, cocaine, nicotine, alcohol, tranquillizers, sugar,
caffeine.
Therapy used:
Hypnotherapy.
Cost:
Between £120 and £150 for complete treatment.

Midland Hypnotherapy Centre
10 Balaclava Road, Kings Heath, Birmingham B14 7SG
Tel: 021 444 5435

Addictions treated:
Heroin, cocaine, nicotine, alcohol, tranquillizers, sugar,
caffeine.
Therapy used:
Hypnotherapy.
Cost:
Course of treatment: Between £120 and £150
First consultation: £20
Subsequent consultation: £15

The Birmingham Centre for Alternative Medicine
16 Poplar Road, Kings Heath, Birmingham, West Midlands
B14 7AD
Tel: 021 443 5516

Addictions treated:
Nicotine, alcohol, tranquillizers.
Therapies used:
Acupuncture, hypnotherapy.
Cost:
Between £15 and £25 per treatment.

Herbal Treatment Centre
68 Sandhurst Road, Moseley, Birmingham B13
Tel: 021 449 4213

Addictions treated:
Tranquillizers, caffeine, sugar.

Therapy used:
Herbal medicine.
Cost:
Consultations: between £4 and £8
Medicines: £2.50 per week.

The Clinic
Suite 433, Gloucester House, Smallbrook, Queensway,
Birmingham B5 4HP
Tel: 021 643 7515

Addictions treated:
Nicotine, tranquillizers.
Therapies used:
Hypnotherapy, psychotherapy.
Cost:
Between £15 and £30 per session.

The Natural Health Centre
38 Hill Street, Coventry, West Midlands
Tel: 0203 29982

Addictions treated:
Nicotine, alcohol, tranquillizers, sugar, caffeine.
Therapies used:
Herbal medicine, diet, massage.
Cost:
£12 per treatment.

Holistic Health Centre
119 Hagley Road, Stourbridge, West Midlands DY8 1RD
Tel: 0384 379740

Addictions treated:
Heroin, nicotine, tranquillizers, sugar, caffeine.
Therapies used:
Acupuncture, homoeopathy, Bach flower remedies, healing.
Cost:
£20 per hour.

Worcestershire

Park Attwod Therapeutic Centre
Trimpley, Bewdley, Worcestershire DY12 1RE
Tel: 02997 444

Addiction treated:
Tranquillizers.
Therapies used:
Anthroposophical medicine – which includes homoeopathy,
massage, diet, herbal medicine, counselling and creative work.
Cost:
Residential. Between £32 and £72 a day.

Yorkshire

The Practitioner
15 Croft Court, Finningley, Doncaster, South Yorkshire
DN9 3PJ
Tel: 0302 771817

Addictions treated:
Heroin, cocaine, tranquillizers, nicotine, alcohol, sugar,
caffeine.
Therapies used:
Hypnotherapy, psychotherapy.
Cost:
First consultation: £10
Subsequent treatment: £25

The Richardson Clinic
Westgate, Heckmondwike, West Yorkshire
Tel: 0924 402763

Addictions treated:
Heroin, cocaine, nicotine, alcohol, tranquillizers, sugar,
caffeine.
Therapies used:
Acupuncture, hypnotherapy, homoeopathic desensitization.
Cost:
Between £11.50 and £25 per treatment.

The Practitioner
24 Vernon Road, Bridlington, Yorkshire YO15 2HE
Tel: 0262 674952

Addictions treated:
Nicotine, tranquillizers.
Therapies used:
Acupuncture, herbal medicine, Bach flower remedies.

Cost:
£10 per session.

The Practitioner
Wood View Farm, Birkby Road, Huddersfield, Yorkshire
HD2 2DN
Tel: 0484 27898

Addictions treated:
Nicotine, alcohol, tranquillizers.
Therapy used:
Hypnotherapy.
Cost:
£50 per course.

The Practitioner
595 Scott Hall Road, Leeds, Yorkshire LS7 2NA
Tel: 0532 681326

Addiction treated:
Nicotine.
Therapy used:
Hypnotherapy.
Cost:
£10 per session.

The Practitioner
3 Troy Road, Morley, Leeds, Yorkshire LS27 0NY
Tel: 0532 533494

Addictions treated:
Nicotine, tranquillizers, alcohol, sugar, caffeine.
Therapy used:
Hypnotherapy.
Cost:
First consultation: £30
Subsequent sessions: £15

The Practitioner
Garrow Way, Garrow Hill, York YO1 3HL
Tel: 0904 412337

Addictions treated:
Alcohol, nicotine, tranquillizers, sugar, caffeine.
Therapies used:
Hypnotherapy, psychotherapy, relaxation, reflexology, healing.

Cost:
£15 per session.

Ireland

The Acupuncture Clinic
Dillons Cross, Cork, Ireland.
Tel: 021 341322

Addictions treated:
Alcohol, nicotine.
Therapy used:
Acupuncture.
Cost:
Tobacco acupuncture course: £20
Alcohol acupuncture course: £100

Holistic Therapies Clinic
9 Westcourt, Caherslee, Tralee, Ireland.
Tel: 066 24694 (local calls)

Addictions treated:
Tranquillizers, nicotine, alcohol, sugar.
Therapies used:
Acupuncture, homoeopathy, meditation, nutrition.
Cost:
First treatment: £17
Subsequent treatments: £12

Down

North Down Clinic for Osteopathy and Alternative Medicine
15 Farnham Road, Bangor, County Down BT20 3SP Northern
Ireland.
Tel: 0247 270626

Addictions treated:
Nicotine, alcohol, tranquillizers.
Therapy used:
Cranial osteopathy.
Cost:
£20 per session.

Scotland

The Clinic
71 Maybole Road, Ayr, Ayrshire, Scotland KA7 4TB
Tel: 0292 43346

Addictions treated:
Tranquillizers, nicotine, alcohol, sugar, caffeine.
Therapy used:
Acupuncture, homoeopathy, herbal medicine, iridology, allergy
testing.
Cost:
£8 per treatment.

Auchenkyle Healing Centre,
Southwoods Road, Troon, Ayrshire, Scotland.
Tel: 0292 311414

Addictions treated:
Heroin, cocaine, alcohol, nicotine, tranquillizers, sugar,
caffeine.
Therapies used:
Acupuncture, visualization (a form of meditation), herbal
medicine, homoeopathy.
Cost:
£10 per consultation

Herbal Treatment Clinic
4 Abercorn Road, Edinburgh EH8 7DE
Tel: 031 652 1376

Addictions treated:
Alcohol, nicotine, tranquillizers, sugar, caffeine.
Therapies used:
Medical herbalism, counselling, nutrition, exercise, relaxation.
Cost:
First consultation: £15
Subsequent consultations vary in cost.
Medicine: about £2 a week.

The Clinic
12 Hartington Place, Edinburgh EH10 4LE
Tel: 031 229 2705

Addictions treated:
Alcohol, tranquillizers, sugar, caffeine.
Therapies used:
Homoeopathy, nutrition.
Cost:
£15 per session or £30 for two months' treatment.

The Christian Fellowship of Healing (Scotland)
Holy Corner Church Centre, 15 Morningside Road, Edinburgh
EH10 4DP
Tel: 031 447 9383

Addictions treated:
'We come across most of the addictions you list and have our successes and our failures.'
Therapies used:
'Prayer, meditation, the Sacraments and the continued upholding fellowship of availability.'
Cost:
No charge; donations accepted.

Edinburgh Homoeopathic Centre and Clinic Ltd
4b Randolph Place, Edinburgh EH3 7TC
Tel: 031 225 1875

Addictions treated:
Nicotine, tranquillizers, alcohol, sugar.
Therapies used:
Acupuncture, herbal medicine, homoeopathy, diet, counselling, nutrition.
Cost:
First consultation: between £20 and £30
Subsequent consultations: between £12 and £15

The Herbal Treatment Centre
41 Balcastle Gardens, Kilsyth, Glasgow G65 9PE
Tel: 0236 824 813

Addictions treated:
Nicotine, tranquillizers, sugar, caffeine.
Therapies used:
Medical herbalism, reflex zone therapy (treating the whole person by treating the feet), diet, astrological counselling.

Cost:
First consultation (one hour): £12
Subsequent consultations (half an hour): £6
Medicines: £2 to £3 per week
Astrological consultation: £6 to £25

The Buckingham Clinic
24 Buckingham Terrace, Glasgow G12 8ED
Tel: 041 339 4340

Addiction treated:
Nicotine.
Therapy used:
Acupuncture.
Cost:
£8 per session.

Centre for Stress Relief, Education and Research in Scotland
2 Royal Terrace, Glasgow G3 7NT
Tel: 041 332 0644

Addictions treated:
Heroin, cocaine, nicotine, alcohol, tranquillizers.
Therapies used:
Hypnotherapy and self-hypnosis, Metamorphic technique
(a whole-person treatment using the feet), relaxation and
breathing.
Cost:
Between £10 and £20 a session.

The Clinic
'Mansewood', New Luce, Newton Stewart, Wigtownshire
DG8 0AL
Tel: 05816 281

Addictions treated:
Tranquillizers, caffeine.
Therapies used:
Breathing, yoga, meditation, visualization.
Cost:
Between £10 and £15 per session.

Wales

The Practitioner
8 Penllwynrhodyn, Llwynhendy, Llanelli, Dyfed, Wales
SA14 9NL
Tel: 0554 757194

Addictions treated:
Nicotine, alcohol, tranquillizers, sugar, caffeine.
Therapies used:
Healing, counselling, nutrition, yoga, breathing and meditation, relaxation.
Cost:
First consultation: Between £15 and £20
Subsequent sessions: £10 to £15

Llanelli Clinic of Natural Therapy
46 Thomas Street, Llanelli, Dyfed, Wales
Tel: 0554 751684

Addictions treated:
Nicotine, alcohol, tranquillizers, sugar, caffeine.
Therapies used:
Clinical kinesiology (diagnosis using touch), homoeopathy, herbal medicine, nutrition and supplements, acupuncture.
Cost:
First consultation: £18
Subsequent treatments: £13

The Practitioner
1 Alexandra Place, Sirhowy, Tredegar, Gwent, Wales
Tel: 049425 2931

Addictions treated:
Alcohol, nicotine, tranquillizers, sugar.
Therapies used:
Hypnotherapy, psychotherapy and counselling, Applied kinesiology (diagnosis through touch), homoeopathy, biofeedback (self-regulation).
Cost:
Between £12.50 and £15 per session.

Bridgend Clinic of Natural Therapy
9b Adare Street, Bridgend, Mid-Glamorgan, Wales
Tel: 0656 645177

Addictions treated:
Nicotine, alcohol, tranquillizers, sugar, caffeine.
Therapies used:
Clinical kinesiology (diagnosis using touch), homoeopathy,
herbal medicine, nutrition and supplements, acupuncture.
Cost:
First consultation: £18
Subsequent treatments: £15

The Herbal Clinic
32 King Edward's Road, Swansea, West Glamorgan SA1 4LL
Tel: 0792 474356

Addictions treated:
Tranquillizers, nicotine, alcohol, sugar.
Therapy used:
Medical herbalism.
Cost:
First consultation: £20
Subsequent consultations: £15
Medicines: Between £5 and £15 per fortnight.

Index